VOLLEYBALL

Steps to Success

Barbara L. Viera, MS
Bonnie Jill Ferguson, MS
University of Delaware, Newark

Leisure Press
Champaign, Illinois

Library of Congress Cataloging-in-Publication Data

Viera, Barbara L., 1941-
    Volleyball: steps to success / Barbara L. Viera, Bonnie Jill Ferguson.
        p.   cm. — (Steps to success activity series)
    ISBN 0-88011-315-4
    1. Volleyball. I. Ferguson, Bonnie Jill, 1957-   . II. Title.
III. Series.
GV1015.3.V54   1989   88-2448
796.32'5—dc19

Developmental Editor: Judy Patterson Wright, PhD
Production Director: Ernie Noa
Copy Editor: Peter Nelson
Assistant Editors: Kathy Kane and Robert King
Proofreader: Laurie McGee
Typesetter: Sonnie Bowman
Text Design: Keith Blomberg
Text Layout: Tara Welsch
Cover Design: Jack Davis
Cover Photo: Bill Morrow
Illustrations By: Sharon Barner and Gretchen Walters
Printed By: United Graphics, Inc.

Instructional Designer for the Steps to Success Activity Series: Joan N. Vickers, EdD

ISBN: 0-88011-315-4

Printed in the United States of America

10 9 8 7 6

Leisure Press
A Division of Human Kinetics Publishers, Inc.
Box 5076, Champaign, IL 61825-5076
1-800-747-4457

Canada Office:
Human Kinetics Publishers, Inc.
P.O. Box 2503, Windsor, ON N8Y 4S2
1-800-465-7301 (in Canada only)

Europe Office:
Human Kinetics Publishers (Europe) Ltd.
P.O. Box IW14
Leeds LS16 6TR
England
0532-781708

Contents

Series Preface

The Steps to Success Activity Series is a breakthrough in skill instruction through the development of complete learning progressions—the *steps to success*. These *steps* help students quickly perform basic skills successfully and prepare them to acquire advanced skills readily. At each step, students are encouraged to learn at their own pace and to integrate their new skills into the total action of the activity, which motivates them to achieve.

The unique features of the Steps to Success Activity Series are the result of comprehensive development—through analyzing existing activity books, incorporating the latest research from the sport sciences, and consulting with students, instructors, teacher educators, and administrators. This groundwork pointed up the need for three different types of books—for participants, instructors, and teacher educators—which we have created and together comprise the Steps to Success Activity Series.

The *participant book* for each activity is a self-paced, step-by-step guide; learners can use it as a primary resource for a beginning activity class or as a self-instructional guide. The unique features of each *step* in the participant book include

- sequential illustrations that clearly show proper technique for all basic skills,
- helpful suggestions for detecting and correcting errors,
- excellent drill progressions with accompanying *Success Goals* for measuring performance, and
- a complete checklist for each basic skill for a trained observer to rate the learner's technique.

A comprehensive *instructor guide* accompanies the participant's book for each activity, emphasizing how to individualize instruction. Each *step* of the instructor's guide promotes successful teaching and learning with

- teaching cues (*Keys to Success*) that emphasize fluidity, rhythm, and wholeness,

- criterion-referenced rating charts for evaluating a participant's initial skill level,
- suggestions for observing and correcting typical errors,
- tips for group management and safety,
- ideas for adapting every drill to increase or decrease the difficulty level,
- quantitative evaluations for all drills (*Success Goals*), and
- a complete test bank of written questions.

The series textbook, *Instructional Design for Teaching Physical Activities*, explains the *steps to success* model, which is the basis for the Steps to Success Activity Series. Teacher educators can use this text in their professional preparation classes to help future teachers and coaches learn how to design effective physical activity programs in school, recreation, or community teaching and coaching settings.

After identifying the need for participant, instructor, and teacher educator texts, we refined the *steps to success* instructional design model and developed prototypes for the participant and the instructor books. Once these prototypes were fine-tuned, we carefully selected authors for the activities who were not only thoroughly familiar with their sports but also had years of experience in teaching them. Each author had to be known as a gifted instructor who understands the teaching of sport so thoroughly that he or she could readily apply the *steps to success* model.

Next, all of the participant and instructor manuscripts were carefully developed to meet the guidelines of the *steps to success* model. Then our production team, along with outstanding artists, created a highly visual, user-friendly series of books.

The result: The Steps to Success Activity Series is the premier sports instructional series available today. The participant books are the best available for helping you to become a master player, the instructor guides will help you to become a master teacher, and the teacher educator's text prepares you to design your own programs.

This series would not have been possible without the contributions of the following:

- Dr. Joan Vickers, instructional design expert,
- Dr. Rainer Martens, Publisher,
- the staff of Human Kinetics Publishers,
- the following volleyball teachers and coaches who, as recognized outstanding volleyball teachers by their colleagues, helped shape this book and others in the series with their questionnaire responses: Barbara Viera, Bonnie Jill Ferguson, Annalies Knoppers, Connie Fox, Sandy Gibbons, Leigh Goldie, Laurel and John Kessel, Sandy Stewart, March Krotee, Diane Jacoby, JoAnn Atwell-Scrivner, Patricia Sheldon, M. Elizabeth Verner, Carl McGowen, Scott McQuilkin, Debbie Holzapfel, Peggy Rees, Walter Versen, Stew McDole, Nancy Chapman, Jody Clasey, Dorothy Wells, and
- the *many* students, teachers, coaches, consultants, teacher educators, specialists, and administrators who shared their ideas—and dreams.

Judy Patterson Wright
Series Editor

Preface

Although volleyball was invented in the United States, not until recently has our country assumed a leadership role in its development. As is true in most sports, the key to player development is learning correct technique early on. This book has been written to introduce you to the game of volleyball and its skills and strategies. You will improve your skills more quickly by understanding the correct method of performance and why each skill is important in a competitive setting.

The Steps to Success model allows you to progress at your own pace as you practice the skills within drills that simulate game situations as closely as possible. While you practice the basic skills, you will learn the key phrases and concepts for correct performance. Once you have mastered the drill goals, it will be easy to adapt to competitive match play. And as you improve your level of performance, you'll enjoy the game more and more.

As in any project of this magnitude, many people have contributed to its successful completion. We would like to thank Karen Woodie for the help she has rendered in word processing and computer technology; David Barlow, PhD, for his help in the filming presented to the artist for sketching diagrams; and our subjects, Jeanne Dyson, Nancy Griskowitz, Maggie Hennigan, Sue Sowter, Pat Castagno, John Aiello, and Clare Wisniewski. We would also like to extend our sincere appreciation to Sharon Barner and Gretchen Walters, who transformed photos and diagrams into expert drawings.

We would like to thank each other for sharing ideas and for the patience necessary to complete this book. Finally, we are very grateful to the people around us for their support and understanding.

Barbara L. Viera
Bonnie Jill Ferguson

The Steps to Success Staircase

Get ready to climb a staircase—one that will lead you to be a great volleyball player. You cannot leap to the top; you get there by climbing one step at a time.

Each of the 24 steps you are about to take is an easy transition from the one before. The first few steps of the staircase provide a foundation—a solid foundation of basic skills and concepts. As you progress further, you will learn how to connect groups of those seemingly isolated skills. Practicing common combinations of volleyball skills will give you the experience you need to begin making natural and accurate decisions on the court. You will learn to make the right moves in various game situations—whether you're serving or receiving, spiking or blocking. As you near the top of the staircase, the climb will ease, and you'll find that you have developed a sense of confidence in your volleyball playing ability that makes further progress a real joy.

Familiarize yourself with this section as well as the sections "The Game of Volleyball" and "Preparing Your Body for Success" for an orientation and in order to understand how to set up your practice sessions around the steps.

Follow the same sequence each step (chapter) of the way:

1. Read the explanations of what is covered in the step, why the step is important, and how to execute or perform the step's focus, which may be a basic skill, concept, tactic, or combination of them.
2. Follow the numbered illustrations showing exactly how to position your body to execute each basic skill successfully. There are three general parts to each skill description: preparation phase (getting into a starting position), execution phase (performing the skill that is the focus of the step), and follow-through phase (recovering back to the starting position).
3. Look over the common errors that may occur and the recommendation of how to correct them.
4. The drills help you improve your skills through repetition and purposeful practice. Read the directions and the Success Goal for each drill. Practice accordingly. Most drills require players in different positions; be sure to switch positions in order to practice all aspects of each drill. Record your score. Compare your score with the Success Goal for the drill. You need to meet the Success Goal of each drill before moving on to practice the next one because the drills are arranged in an easy-to-difficult progression. This sequence is designed specifically to help you achieve continual success.
5. As soon as you can reach all the Success Goals for one step, you are ready for a qualified observer—such as your teacher, coach, or trained partner—to evaluate your basic skill technique against the Keys to Success Checklist. This is a qualitative, or subjective, evaluation of your basic technique or form—because using correct form enhances your performance. Your evaluator can tailor specific goals for you, if they are needed, by using the Individual Program form (see the Appendix).
6. Repeat these procedures for each of the 24 Steps to Success. Then rate yourself according to the directions for "Rating Your Game Success."

Good luck on your step-by-step journey to enhancing your volleyball skills, building confidence, experiencing success, and having fun!

KEY

C = coach

$\overset{o}{x}$ = player with ball

x = player

--> = path of ball

——➤ = path of player

△ = target player

⌒ = rolled ball

s = setter

T = tosser

⊢ = box, chair, or official's stand

[feeder box] = feeder

RB = right back

CB = center back

LB = left back

RF = right forward

CF = center forward

LF = left forward

The Game of Volleyball

In 1895 William C. Morgan, a YMCA director in Holyoke, Massachusetts, invented a game called *mintonette* in an attempt to meet the needs of local businessmen who found the game of basketball to be too strenuous. The new game caught on quickly because it required only a few basic skills, easily mastered in limited practice time and by players of varying fitness levels. The original game was played with a rubber bladder from a basketball. Early rules allowed any number of players on a side. In 1896 the name was changed by Alfred T. Halstead, who, after viewing a game, felt that *volleyball* would be a more suitable name due to the volleying characteristic of play.

As the game has progressed, many changes in play have occurred. For example, the Filipinos are credited with adding the spike.

The game's status has changed from its being a recreational activity to being recognized as a strenuous sport as well. The Japanese added the sport to the Olympic Games program in 1964; this contributed to the fast growth of volleyball in the last 25 years.

The exciting aspect of volleyball is that it attracts all types of players—recreational to competitive, little skilled to highly skilled—and all ages. The game has great appeal because it requires few basic skills, few rules, few players (from two to six players on a side), and limited equipment, and it can be played on a variety of surfaces, from a hardwood floor to a sandy beach.

PLAYING A GAME

The game of volleyball is played by two teams each having two to six players on a 30-foot square (9-meter square) court, the two courts separated by a net. The primary objective of each team is to try to hit the ball to the opponent's side in such a manner as to prevent the opponent from returning the ball. This is usually accomplished by using a three-hit combination of a forearm pass to a setter, followed by a set to an attacker, who spikes the ball into the opponent's court.

When there are six players on a side, three are called *forwards*, and three are called *backs*. The three players in the front row are called *left forward* (LF), *center forward* (CF), and *right forward* (RF). The three players in the back row are called *left back* (LB), *center back* (CB), and *right back* (RB). Players need to be in their correct *rotational positions* until the serve is executed. This means that players cannot overlap positions from front to back or from side to side (see Figure A). After the serve, players are allowed to play in any position on or off the court, with one restriction: back row players cannot leave the floor to hit the ball when in front of the attack line. A side out

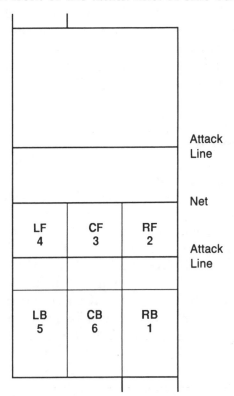

Figure A Players arranged in proper rotational positions.

occurs when a team that is not serving wins the rally. When a team earns a side out, they rotate clockwise one position (see Figure B).

All this requires that each player must master the intricacies of every one of the positions. This interesting aspect of volleyball differentiates it from other team sports. As the game of volleyball becomes more competitive, players are finding it increasingly difficult to learn the in-depth characteristics of all six positions. Therefore, the *specialization* of players is commonly found. When players specialize, they switch to the same area of the court (left, center, or right) as soon as the serve is executed. These positions are referred to as their *playing positions*.

The serve is initiated by the right back player from a position behind the end line (see Figure C). A team scores points only while it is serving, and the same player continues to serve as long as the serving team wins each rally. A rally is the continuous play of the ball over the net between opponents, ending in a point or side out. A point is awarded each time your team serves the ball and wins the rally. A game consists of at least 15 points, and a team must be two points ahead to win. A match in volleyball consists of best 2 out of 3 or 3 out of 5 games.

RULES

Currently volleyball in the United States is being played under three sets of rules. Basically, most high schools play under the rules of the National Federation of State High School Associations; college women play under the National Association of Girls and Women in Sport (NAGWS); college men, all recreational, and club teams play under the United States Volleyball Association (USVBA). International Rules govern all competition between nations. In recent years, all four sets of rules are approaching uniformity. The USVBA and NAGWS are identical except for substitution rules. For the purposes of this book, our discussion is based upon NAGWS rules.

It is important that all players be familiar with the court markings. The volleyball court is 59 feet (18 meters) long and 29 feet 6 inches

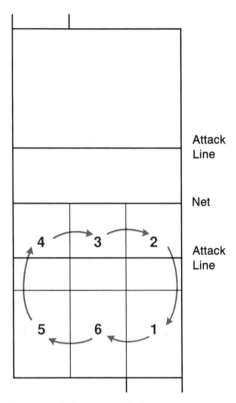

Figure B Rotational direction of players on a side-out.

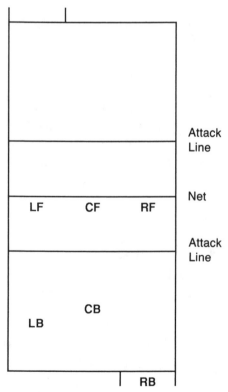

Figure C Position of serving team members during serve.

(9 meters wide), marked by sidelines, and end lines, respectively. Other lines of importance on a court consist of

- the *centerline*, dividing the court into two equal playing areas, sometimes known as *courts* themselves, or *sides*;
- the *attack line*, parallel to, and 9 feet 10 inches (3 meters) from, the centerline;
- the *serving area*, the right one third of the court outside the end line, with a minimum depth of 6 feet. If this required space does not exist, a player, on the service, is allowed to step into the court up to the distance needed to make up the difference (see Figure D).

The correct height of the net for women is 7 feet 4-1/8 inches (2.24 meters); for men or coed play, 7 feet 11-5/8 inches (2.43 meters).

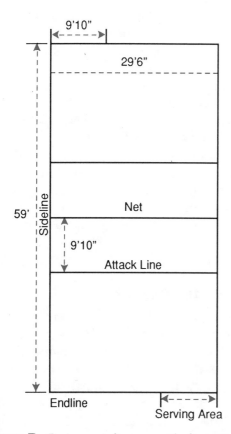

Figure D Basic court diagram with dimensions.

The legal portion of the net is the part between the sidelines of the court.

A match begins with a coin toss between the teams' captains. The captain who wins the toss may either choose first service for that team or select the playing side. The other captain gets the remaining choice. The first serve rights alternate with each game until the deciding game of the match, at which time a second toss is made. Teams change sides at eight points in the deciding game. However, if both captains agree not to change (at the coin toss prior to that game), they may continue on the same side.

A team consists of six players on the court at all times. A squad cannot exceed 12 players. The lineup at the beginning of the game determines the service order throughout the game. Players of both teams must be in their correct rotational order at the time of the service by either team. The correct position of each player is described as follows:

- In the front line, the center forward must be between the right forward and the left forward, and in front of the center back.
- In the back line, the center back must be between the right back and the left back, and behind the center forward.
- The right forward must be in front of the right back, and the left forward must be in front of the left back.

When a player is out of position, play is stopped, the error is corrected, points scored while the team was in error are canceled, and a point or a side out is awarded to the opponents.

The player in the right back position has 5 seconds to initiate the serve from the service area. The server must use one hand—either open or closed—or the arm to make contact. The ball may not touch the net and must be over the legal portion of the net. If a bad toss is made, the server may let the ball drop to the floor without touching it and begin again, being allowed an additional 5 seconds for a second attempt. The server may not step on or over the end line until after the ball is contacted.

The following rules govern contacting the ball during play:

- Each team is allowed a maximum of three successive contacts in order to return the ball to the opponent's area. If the first touch is on a block, the team may have three additional contacts to return the ball. In effect, the touch on the block does not count.
- The ball may contact any part of the body above and including the waist.
- The ball may contact any number of body parts as long as it does so simultaneously.
- When the ball comes to rest momentarily in the hand or arms of a player, it is considered *held*.
- With the exception of a blocker, *double contact* is when one person hits the ball more than once with no other person touching it between these contacts.
- If the ball is held simultaneously by two opposing players, it is a *double fault* and results in a playover.
- If two players on the same team contact the ball simultaneously (both must physically touch the ball), this is considered as two contacts for their team.
- When two opponents commit a fault simultaneously, a playover must occur.
- A player who places any part of the body above the height of the net is considered to have the intention to block; only front line players may block.
- If two players contact the ball on the block, it is considered as only one hit.
- Blockers may reach over the net to block the ball as long as the opponents have hit the ball in such a manner that the ball would clearly cross the net if not touched by a defending player.

Several rules govern play near the net and at the centerline:

- The ball remains in play if it touches the legal portion of the net in play, other than on the serve.
- A player may not touch the net while the ball is in play.

- If the ball is driven into the net with such force that it contacts an opponent, this is not a net fault.
- The hands may legally pass over the net after a spike on the follow-through.
- The only parts of the body allowed to touch the opponent's court are a foot or the feet; however, some part of the foot or feet must remain on or above the centerline at the time of contact.
- You can cross the *vertical plane* (an imaginary continuation of the net above and below its actual limits) of the net as long as you don't interfere with the opponent.
- Once the ball is *dead*, it is not a fault to hit the net or cross over the centerline. A ball is dead when it has touched the playing surface, when it is ruled out-of-bounds, or when a rally has ended due to an official's whistle.
- A player may not spike the ball until part of the ball is on that player's side of the net.

Only forwards are permitted to spike or to return the ball with their hands in a position higher than the top of the net from in front of the attack line. Back line players may not block and may spike only when they take off (jump) from behind the attack line.

The ball must pass from one side of the net to the other over the legal portion of the net. A ball landing on a boundary line is considered to be in the court. A player may go off the court to play a ball. A ball coming from the opponents that is perceived to be out-of-bounds may not be caught until it legally touches an out-of-bounds area.

VOLLEYBALL TODAY

Volleyball is a sport that is played in most countries around the world. "In 1970 a survey taken on behalf of the International Olympic Committee reported that volleyball and basketball were equal, with approximately 65 million registered players in each sport" (International Federal Coaches Manual, p. 1.2). The popularity of the game was enhanced greatly when the Japanese added it to the Olympic Games program in 1964.

Interestingly, although the game was invented in the United States, it was not until the mid-1980s that the Americans began to provide strong leadership for its development. In 1984, for the first time ever, the United States' men's and women's teams won Olympic medals. The United States' men defeated Brazil to capture the gold, and the United States' women lost to China in the finals to capture the silver. The success of these two teams has increased the interest level of volleyball throughout the United States from both participants' and spectators' points of view.

Characteristics of the game enable participants to enjoy it regardless of their ability levels. Whether it be played as a backyard picnic game in which anything goes or a highly competitive match between two national teams, the game is quick, powerful, exciting, and challenging. Volleyball can be considered a lifetime sport. It can be adapted to all age groups and levels of play. Presently, it is an extremely popular recreational activity with numerous leagues in business, community, and school intramural programs. At the United States Volleyball Championships each year, in addition to the Open Champions, winners are also recognized in the Senior (female 30 years and older, male 35 and up) and the Golden Masters (males 45 and up) divisions. These two groups being determined by the ages of the participants allows players to continue at the highest level of competitiveness possible as their ages increase.

In addition to organized competition of all types, volleyball continues to be one of the most popular sports played at social gatherings. The type of game played on these occasions can be low in skill level, utilizing a few simple rules and enjoyed by all.

On the professional level, volleyball is currently played in several foreign countries with financial success. However, in the United States, the first professional league struggled financially and eventually folded in 1982. An interesting aspect of this league was that its teams were coeducational. Although men and women assumed differing roles during the match (women played defensive positions while the men assumed predominantly offensive responsibilities), success came from the overall team effort. In 1987, a new women's volleyball league (Major League Volleyball) was established. This league's players were paid, but the league was not considered *professional* in the true sense of the word, allowing the players to maintain their amateur option. At this time, the financial future of this enterprise is unknown. It appears that the success of professional volleyball in the United States will depend upon spectator interest. With the number of participants in volleyball increasing on a yearly basis at all levels, it would seem that the new women's league will have a better chance at success than the original professional league.

With the impetus of the 1984 Olympic success of our American national teams, volleyball continues to grow and develop in the United States at all levels of play. The financial success of the game depends upon improving the sport's image on the spectator level. This will happen when volleyball is more visible through the media, including newspapers, magazines, and television.

Under the current scoring system in volleyball, the length of a match can vary from 1 hour to more than 3 hours. This depends on how close the participating teams are in ability. This variance in time causes great consternation for the media, particularly television. Various studies have been done on different systems of scoring and time regulations that would make the game more predictable in length. Due to this problem, matches on television are not currently seen in their entirety. A change in the present scoring system and/or the addition of timing regulations may make volleyball more attractive for media coverage.

Three governing bodies currently provide rules for volleyball competitions in the United States. Men's and women's open and men's collegiate competitions use United States Volleyball Association (USVBA) rules. For rules information and interpretation contact the USVBA office: 1750 East Boulder Street, Colorado Springs, CO 80909.

All collegiate women's play and some scholastic girls' competitions are governed by the National Association for Girls and Women in Sport (NAGWS) rules. For rules information and interpretation contact the NAGWS office: 1900 Association Drive, Reston, VA 22091.

The majority of girls' high school play and all boys' high school play is governed by the National Federation of State High School Associations (NFSHSA). For rules information and interpretation contact the NFSHSA office: 11724 Plaza Circle, Box 20626, Kansas City, MO 64195.

The USVBA controls all open play in the United States. The country is divided into regions, with each region responsible for the competitive schedule for its membership. The national office in Colorado Springs can be contacted to obtain information about your regional commissioner. All commissioners have information regarding registration, player eligibility, and tournament schedules. Most regions are now also sponsoring competition for junior players.

Collegiate competition for both men and women is controlled by the National Collegiate Athletic Association (NCAA), the National Association for Intercollegiate Athletics (NAIA), or the National Junior College Athletic Association (NJCAA). These organizations oversee seasonal play and administer both national championships. Questions concerning player eligibility, national championship format, recruiting rules, and so forth should be directed to the appropriate governing body:

NCAA
Nall Avenue at 63rd Street
P.O. Box 1906
Mission, KS 66201

NAIA
1221 Baltimore
Kansas City, MO 64105

NJCAA
P.O. Box 7305
Colorado Springs, CO 80933

The American Volleyball Coaches' Association (AVCA) provides opportunities for coaches at all levels to share ideas and actively promote the game of volleyball. This organization also publishes a bimonthly journal, "Coaching Volleyball," which contains new ideas and current trends in the sport. This journal is a benefit of membership in the AVCA. For more information contact the AVCA office: 122 Second Avenue, Suite 217, San Mateo, CA 94401.

Preparing Your Body for Success

There is a recommended volleyball workout sequence to follow. Prior to practicing, you need a 5- to 10-minute warm-up to increase your heart rate and your flexibility. After finishing your practice, end with a 5-minute cool-down period. Use this time to bring your heart rate down and stretch the muscles used most during your practice. If you follow this sequence, you will not only help prepare your body and mind to play volleyball but also help prevent injuries.

A TWO-PHASE WARM-UP PERIOD

Your first goal is to select and complete one exercise that "gets your blood moving." Then, select one exercise per body part listed under the "Flexibility Exercises." You will get a head-to-toe warm-up as you complete the Flexibility Exercises selected.

Exercises to Get Your Blood Moving

1. Partner Ball Exchange Exercise: Starting on the end line of the court with one volleyball, you run forward as quickly as possible in a medium body posture (easy stride, knees bent so they are ahead of the feet, and shoulders forward ahead of the knees) to the attack line, placing the ball on the line. Turn and run back to the end line, tagging your partner. The partner (medium body posture) runs to the attack line, picks up the ball, and returns to the end line, handing the ball to you. Continue this same running pattern going to the centerline, the attack line on the opposite court, and the opposite end line. The entire sequence should be completed 3 times.
2. Court Perimeter Exercise: Start at the right back corner of the court and run to the net in a medium body posture. When arriving at the net, use sliding steps to move along the net, executing four block jumps. At the left sideline,

backpedal to the end line. At the end line, move to the starting position by using the cross step (cross foot 1 in front of foot 2, step with foot 2 in the direction you are moving and continue to repeat this sequence) with the crossing action in front of your feet only. Repeat all this 3 times.

Flexibility Exercises

The purpose of the flexibility exercises is to stretch the muscles that will be used in the performance of volleyball skills. The best method for increasing flexibility is to stretch a muscle and remain in the stretched position 5–7 seconds. The test for sufficient stretch is that you should feel the stretch of your muscle in the holding position.

Head

1. Head Circles: In a standing or sitting position, slowly make a large circle with your head, lowering it to your chest, moving it to one shoulder, moving it back to the normal, upright position, and moving it toward the other shoulder. Do not allow your head to drop backward during this exercise, because it may lead to injury. Repeat 2 times counterclockwise and 2 times clockwise.

Arms

1. Arm Circles: From a starting position of both arms over your head, slowly circle your arms completely around close to the body and back to the starting position. Repeat 5 times clockwise and 5 times counterclockwise.

2. Behind Back Reach: Reach back with your spiking arm over the shoulder on the same side. Grab your opposite hand behind your back, holding for 5–7 seconds. Repeat twice on both sides.

Back

1. Reach and Stretch: With arms extended and hands joined above your head, reach to the left and hold for 5–7 seconds, making sure that your shoulders and hips face forward. Reach to the right and hold 5–7 seconds. Reach back, arching your back, and hold 5–7 seconds. Repeat 3 times.

2. Floor Stretch: In a prone position on the floor with your arms stretched above your head, lift your upper body off the floor as high as possible and hold for 7 seconds. Repeat 5 times.

Legs

1. Straddle Stretch: Sitting on the floor with your legs apart in a straddle position, your toes pointed toward the ceiling, and your arms overhead, reach forward toward your right ankle. Attempt to place your forehead on your right knee, holding for 7 seconds. Repeat over left leg. Repeat reaching forward between the legs. Repeat sequence 2 times, then repeat twice with toes pointed.

Feet

1. Ankle Circle: Sitting on the floor with your legs straight out in front, slowly move only your feet in a circular pattern, making as large a circle as possible. Repeat 2 clockwise and 2 counter-clockwise foot movements.

2. Crossed Leg Stretch: Standing with legs straight (not hyperextended) and crossed, reach forward, touching your palms to the floor. Hold for 7 seconds. Repeat 3 times.

2. Plant and Roll: In a standing position with feet flat on the floor, slowly roll weight onto your heels, raising your toes off the floor; then roll down onto your toes, raising your heels off the floor. Hold position with your heels off the floor for 7 seconds. Repeat 5 times.

COOL-DOWN PERIOD

When your volleyball activity has been completed, it is best to spend 5 minutes cooling down. During this time, you should choose at least one flexibility exercise for each body part as described for the warm-up. It is recommended that each activity be executed twice through.

The cool-down period is very important because it helps lessen the amount of soreness that you may experience when using and stretching new muscle groups in a new activity.

Step 1 Movement Patterns

When you play volleyball, during the time your feet are in contact with the floor, your body position can be at one of three different levels—high, medium, or low. The high position is basically used for serving, setting, and the starting position for blocking. The medium position is the most important because it is used 70% of the time—during serve reception, the overhead pass, and the starting position for the spike. The low position is used during digging and all forms of individual defense, such as the sprawl and the roll. A fourth body position is your body being in the air; this is used in spiking and blocking.

WHY ARE MOVEMENT PATTERNS IMPORTANT?

It is extremely important that you use the correct body posture for the skill you are about to perform. By using correct posture, you can perform the skill more efficiently, and there is less chance of injury. One example of a common error is when you try performing an individual defensive maneuver from a high posture. If you attempt to do this, you are likely to hit the floor hard due to falling from the high level, thus increasing the chance for injury. When jumping into the air, it is important that your body be balanced before takeoff so that it will be balanced in the air. When landing from an air movement, it is necessary to cushion the landing by bending at your knees, which aids in the prevention of injury.

HOW TO EXECUTE MOVEMENT PATTERNS

High body posture is basically a standing position with your feet in an easy stride, your weight evenly distributed on the balls of your feet (see Figure 1.1a). In the medium posture, your body is in an easy stride with its weight evenly distributed on the balls of your feet, your knees are bent so that they are ahead of your feet, and your shoulders lean forward so that they are in front of your knees. Your hands and arms are above your knees and away from your body (see Figure 1.1b). In the low posture, your weight is forward, your knees are bent more than 90 degrees, and your arms and hands are above your knees and away from your body. When moving to the ball in a low body posture, you must get to the ball before you attempt to play it. You also must make sure that you play the ball before any part of your body, in addition to your feet, contacts the floor, if possible (see Figure 1.1c).

Figure 1.1 Keys to Success: Movement Patterns

High Posture

**Preparation
Phase**

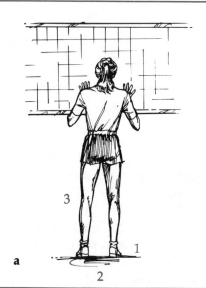

1. Feet shoulder width apart
   a. Side-by-side for blocking
   b. Stride position for other skills
2. Weight evenly distributed
3. Knees slightly bent

**Execution
Phase**

1. Keep same level throughout

**Follow-Through
Phase**

1. Eyes follow ball to target

2. Regain position for next play

Medium Posture

Preparation Phase

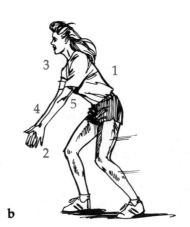

1. Body leans forward
2. Knees in front of feet
3. Shoulders in front of knees
4. Hands and arms above knees
5. Arms away from body

b

Execution Phase

1. Maintain body position during movement
2. Hands are not joined
3. Knees and hips face target
4. End movement with a shuffle-step

Follow-Through Phase

1. Eyes follow ball to target
2. Weight transfers toward target

Low Posture

Preparation Phase

1. Knees bent more than 90 degrees
2. Weight forward

c

Execution Phase

1. Get to ball before playing it
2. Play ball, then hit floor

3. Contact floor with most padded area of body

Follow-Through Phase

1. Eyes follow ball to target

2. Recover for next play

Detecting Movement Pattern Errors

Errors in posture fall into two categories: (a) the selection of the incorrect posture for the skill being performed and (b) selecting the correct posture but executing it poorly. Body postures should be practiced so that they become natural movements to you. You will eventually automatically assume the correct body posture for the skill you anticipate.

ERROR   **CORRECTION**

1. Your hands are too close to your body.	1. Your hands must be far enough away from your body so that your arms are parallel to your thighs.

ERROR   **CORRECTION**

2. You move with your hands joined.

2. Your hands should not be joined during movement, but quickly joined before ball contact.

3. You slam into the floor following a defensive move.

3. Your body must be in a low position and as close to the ball as possible *before* contact.

4. On defense, you do not move through the ball.

4. You must contact the ball and continue by moving toward the target.

Movement Pattern Drills

1. Mirror Drill

The leader stands in front, facing you and the other players. All players are in the medium body posture. The leader moves forward, backward, left, or right. You must follow the leader. Maintain the medium body posture throughout the drill.

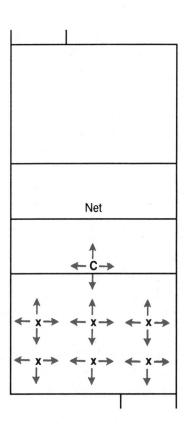

Success Goal = continuous movement for 60 seconds, maintaining the medium body posture

Your Score = (#) _____ seconds maintaining the medium body posture

2. Forward and Backward Movement Drill

Stand in the medium body posture on the attack line, facing the net. With a step-hop, move forward, touch the centerline with your foot, and move back to the attack line.

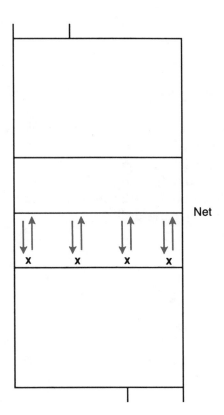

Success Goal = continuous movement with the medium body posture for 30 seconds

Your Score = (#) ____ seconds maintaining the medium body posture

3. Block and Roll Drill

Stand at the net in a high body posture, your elbows bent and close to body, your hands in front of your shoulders. Jump; reach over the net, then quickly withdraw your hands, attempting not to touch the net. Return to the floor in low body posture, sit and roll onto your back, and quickly return to the starting position.

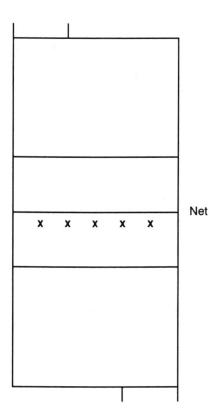

Net

Success Goal = 10 consecutive jumps and rolls without touching the net

Your Score = (#) _____ consecutive jumps and rolls

4. Low to Floor Sit Drill

Begin at the center of the court, facing the net in a low body posture, your hands touching the floor. Maintaining the low posture, slide to the right sideline. At the sideline, take a big step to the side, sit on the floor, then stand and quickly return to the starting position. Repeat this movement to the left. Continue this drill, alternating right and left.

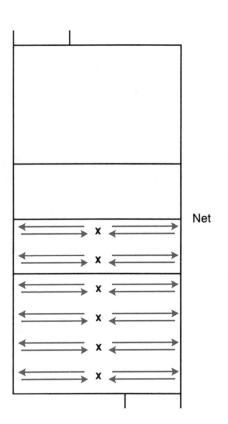

Success Goal = 5 floor sits in 30 seconds

Your Score = (#) _____ floor sits

Movement Patterns
Keys to Success Checklist

When someone observes you for correct body posture, the first question to be answered is, What skill is anticipated? Do you have the correct body posture for the skill to be performed? Once these questions have been answered, your execution can be analyzed. Even though the same high body posture is used for the three different skills—serving, setting, and blocking—the starting positions of the extremities differ. For example, if the block is anticipated, your feet should be side by side, your

hands at shoulder height. If a set is anticipated, though, your feet should be in a stride, with your hands above your forehead. This is true for all body postures—high, medium, and low.

Have a trained observer—your teacher, a coach, a skilled player—watch your movement patterns. The facets below should be checked in the course of your performance. Such an evaluation can help you focus on actions that need extra practice.

High Posture

**Preparation
Phase**

_____ Feet are shoulder width apart.
_____ Weight is evenly distributed on balls
of feet.
_____ Knees are slightly bent.

**Execution
Phase**

_____ Player maintains the correct level
during movement.

**Follow-Through
Phase**

_____ Eyes always follow ball to target.
_____ Player regains starting position quickly for next play.

Medium Posture

Preparation Phase

_____ Body leans forward with the knees in front of the feet, the shoulders in front of the knees.
_____ Hands and arms are above knees, held away from body and parallel to thighs.

Execution Phase

_____ Hands are not joined during movement.
_____ Knees and hips face target.

_____ When player moves in this position, the stopping action is completed with a shuffle-step.

Follow-Through Phase

_____ Weight transfers toward the target.

Low Posture

Preparation Phase

_____ Knees are bent more than 90 degrees.
_____ Body weight is forward.

Execution Phase

_____ Player moves feet and gets to the ball before attempting to play it.
_____ Ball is played prior to player contacting the floor.

_____ Floor is contacted from an extremely low position, with the force of impact being cushioned by the most padded areas of the body.

Follow-Through Phase

_____ Eyes follow ball to target.
_____ Player makes immediate recovery for continuous play.

Step 2 Forearm Pass

The first basic volleyball skill to learn is the forearm pass. This skill is also referred to as the *underhand pass* or the *bump*. It usually is the first skill your team must execute if you have not elected to serve first. It is used to receive serves, receive spikes, play any ball at waist height or lower, and play any ball that has gone into the net.

Although the forearm pass is frequently used, you have better passing control when utilizing the overhead pass (discussed in Step 5). Therefore, if possible, the overhead pass should be your preference. However, any hard-driven ball, that is, a serve or spike, should always be received with a forearm pass because open hands are not strong enough to receive a ball hit with force. The forearm pass is most often used to direct the ball to a teammate. It is important to absorb the force of a hard-hit ball and direct the ball in such a way that your teammate can execute an overhead pass or set on the next play.

WHY IS THE FOREARM PASS IMPORTANT?

As the first skill used when you receive the ball from your opponents, the forearm pass must be executed efficiently if your team is to be successful. As you make the transition from defense to offense, a good forearm pass is essential.

HOW TO EXECUTE THE FOREARM PASS

The basic elements for good execution of the forearm pass are (a) getting to the ball, (b) setting your position, (c) making contact, and (d) following the ball to the target. When performing the forearm pass, your hands must be joined together; your thumbs must be parallel. Your elbows are rotated inward so that the soft, flat portions of your forearms face the ceiling. This *platform* formed by your arms should be as even as possible. Your arms are parallel to your thighs; hold them away from your body. You must try to position your body behind the ball, absorb the force, and direct the ball to the target utilizing your body through leg extension while contacting the ball with little or no arm swing, (poking action). See Figure 2.1 for the forearm pass keys to success.

The forearm pass is a relatively easy skill to perform when you move to the ball first; that is, when you get to the proper position before attempting the skill. The difficulty in the skill is that you probably do not use your forearms in performing any other sport skill. The tendency, therefore, is to hit the ball with the hands; be careful not to acquire this habit.

Figure 2.1 Keys to Success:
Forearm Pass

**Preparation
Phase**

1. Hands must be joined
2. Stride position
3. Feet shoulder width
   apart
4. Knees bent
5. Forearms parallel to
   thighs
6. Back straight
7. Eyes on ball

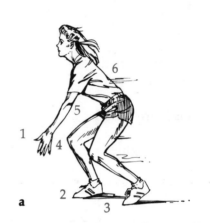

**Execution
Phase**

1. Thumbs parallel
2. Heels of hands together
3. Receive ball on left side
   of body
4. Slight extension of legs
5. Forward and upward
   "poking" motion
6. Platform slanted toward
   target
7. Hips under and forward
8. Watch ball contact arms

**Follow-Through
Phase**

1. Hands remain joined
2. Platform follows ball to target
3. Arms not higher than shoulders
4. Transfer of weight forward
5. Eyes follow ball to target

d

Detecting Forearm Pass Errors

If you learn to recognize the components of correct execution of the forearm pass, it becomes easier for you to analyze your attempts to perform correctly and to analyze the attempts of fellow students as well. The most common forearm pass errors are listed here, along with suggestions on how to correct them.

ERROR

CORRECTION

1. Your arms are too high when you contact the ball. Your arms follow through above shoulder height.

1. Let the ball drop to waist level before contact. Try to stop your arms on contact by using a "poking" action on the ball.

2. You get low by bending at your waist instead of your knees, causing you to pass the ball too low and too fast.

2. Bend your knees, keeping your back straight as you move under the ball; touch the floor with your hands to stay in a low position.

ERROR   **CORRECTION**

3. You do not transfer weight toward the intended target; as a result, the ball does not travel forward.

3. Check that your weight ends up on your forward foot and that your body is inclined forward.

4. Your hands separate before, at, or just after contacting the ball, resulting in an errant pass.

4. Keep your hands joined by interlocking your fingers, or wrapping one hand in the other with thumbs parallel.

ERROR

CORRECTION

The ball contacts your arms at or above your elbows and/or contacts your torso.

5. Keep your arms parallel to your thighs and contact the ball away from your torso.

Forearm Pass Drills

1. Passing a Held Ball Drill

Have a partner loosely hold the ball out toward you at waist level. Using forearm pass technique, hit the ball out of your partner's hands so that it is directed back over your partner's head. Your partner then retrieves the ball, and the drill continues.

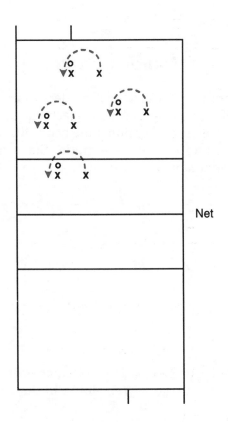

Net

Success Goal = 25 good forearm passes in 30 attempts

Your Score = (#) _____ forearm passes over partner's head

2. Partner Pass Drill

Have a partner toss you a ball; using your fore-arms, pass the ball back to your partner. Your partner must be able to catch your pass without taking more than one step in any direction.

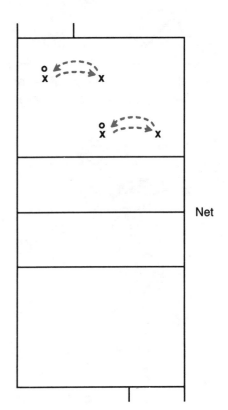

Success Goal = 20 good forearm passes in 25 attempts

Your Score = (#) _____ forearm passes to partner

3. Continuous Bumping Drill

Gently toss a volleyball underhand to yourself and use forearm pass technique to keep the ball in the air. Bump the ball 8–10 feet high by using the net as a guide. Stay within a 10-foot square.

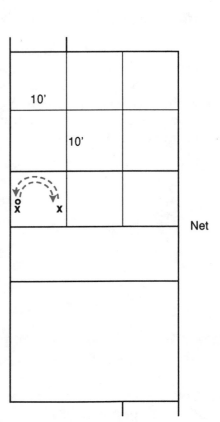

Success Goal = 25 consecutive bumps while remaining in the 10-foot square

Your Score = (#) _____ bumps in a row

4. *Passing to Target Drill*

In a group of three, one person tosses a ball over the net to you. Receive the ball and direct it using a forearm pass to a third person positioned at the net.

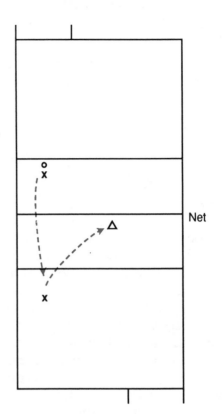

Net

Success Goal = 20 accurate forearm passes out of 25 attempts

Your Score = (#) _____ forearm passes

5. *Pass and Move Drill*

In a group of three, have two partners stand 20 feet apart on the attack line, facing the end line. You are to face the net and move laterally (left and right) to the spots directly in front of the other two players. As you approach one of the spots, the player aligned with it tosses the ball. You receive the ball by forearm passing it back at least 2 feet higher than the height of the net. The tosser should not have to move more than one step in any direction to catch your pass.

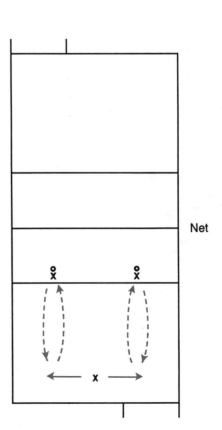

Net

Success Goal = 20 accurate forearm passes out of 25 attempts

Your Score = (#) _____ forearm passes back to the tosser

6. *Forearm Pass for Accuracy Drill*

Have a partner stand on the attack line on one side of the court. You stand near the middle of the end line in the back third of the other side of the court.

Your partner tosses a ball to either side. Move to receive and forearm pass the ball to a 10-foot square target area on your side of the court between the attack line and the center-line. The target should begin 5 feet from the right sideline and extend 10 feet into the center of the court. Your pass should reach a height of 2 feet above the net.

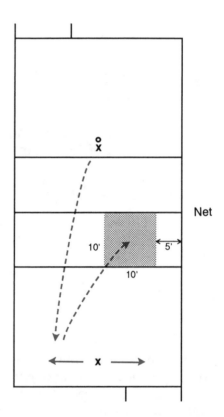

Success Goal = 20 on-target forearm passes out of 25

Your Score = (#) _____ forearm passes to the target area

Forearm Pass
Keys to Success Checklist

When someone checks on your forearm pass technique, the occasional poor pass usually gives a strong indication of the type of error made. For example, if the ball goes straight up from your hands rather than forward, two possible performance errors are indicated: (a) you have not transferred your weight forward, or (b) you have contacted the ball too high. Have someone check your performance for the following points.

**Preparation
Phase**

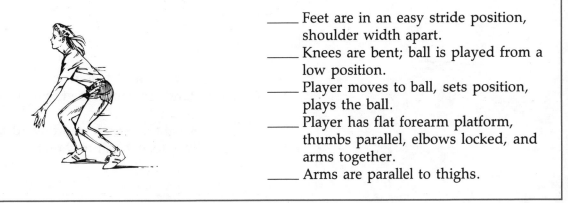

_____ Feet are in an easy stride position, shoulder width apart.

_____ Knees are bent; ball is played from a low position.

_____ Player moves to ball, sets position, plays the ball.

_____ Player has flat forearm platform, thumbs parallel, elbows locked, and arms together.

_____ Arms are parallel to thighs.

Execution
Phase

_____ Player receives the ball on left side of the body.
_____ Arms move forward and upward with little swing.
_____ Weight transfers forward.
_____ Passer directs ball to target.
_____ Ball is contacted away from body for proper trajectory.

Follow-Through
Phase

_____ Arms remain below shoulder level.
_____ Hands remain joined, elbows remain locked.
_____ Weight is transferred toward target.
_____ Eyes follow ball to target.

Step 3 Serve

Your next skill to master is the serve. There are several different types of serves in volleyball. Each one has its advantages and disadvantages. The only time that you earn points in volleyball is when your team is serving. It is therefore very important that you serve with consistency—that is, serve the ball over the net into the opponent's court at least 90% of the time. The serve is the only skill in volleyball in which you have total control during the execution; therefore, you are solely responsible for the result.

Every volleyball player should master the two basic serves—the underhand serve and the overhand floater. The first priority when serving is consistency. Any player can easily serve the ball underhand. Once you are consistent in using the underhand serve, you should practice other serves that are more effective.

The overhand floater serve is the next least complex serve to learn. Do not attempt this serve until you have mastered the underhand serve. The name *floater* is derived from the fact that the ball moves from side to side, or up and down, as it travels across the net. This happens because the ball is hit without spin. Spin stabilizes a ball in flight; without spin, the ball appears to move and jump. This movement is very similar to the ''knuckling'' action of a pitched baseball.

WHY ARE THE UNDERHAND AND THE OVERHAND FLOATER SERVES IMPORTANT?

The serve begins the game. Your team can continue to control the play as long as you maintain the serve. The underhand serve is the easiest one to perform. This serve, although usually easy for opponents to receive, is one that you should perform with total confidence. You should master the underhand serve with 90% consistency before attempting other serves.

The floater serve is initiated from a higher point than the underhand serve. The straighter trajectory that results makes the ball more difficult to receive, because it comes with greater force and takes less time to travel the same distance. These two factors, along with the unpredictable floating action, makes the mastering of this serve an advantage over your opponents.

HOW TO EXECUTE THE UNDERHAND SERVE

The starting position for performing the underhand serve is standing in a stride position with the leg on the side opposite your hitting hand forward and shoulders square to the net. Hold the ball about waist level, slightly to the center from your front foot, with your weight evenly distributed on both feet. Your hitting hand swings backward above waist level and then forward to contact the ball. Your weight shifts with the swing of your hand, shifting to the rear foot and then forward to the front foot. Just prior to contact, your holding hand drops away from the ball. Your hitting hand swings forward and up toward the top of the net. You contact the ball with an open hand, the heel of your hand cutting into the back of the ball just below its center. Watch the flight of your serve and prepare for further action (see Figure 3.1).

Figure 3.1 Keys to Success:
Underhand Serve

**Preparation
Phase**

1. Stride position
2. Ball at waist level
3. Shoulders square to net
4. Eyes on ball
5. Open hitting hand

**Execution
Phase**

1. Arm swings back
2. Weight shifts back
3. Arm swings forward
4. Weight shifts forward
5. "Holding" hand drops ball
6. Use heel of open hand
7. Contact ball at waist level
8. Contact ball below center back of ball

**Follow-Through
Phase**

1. Weight on front foot
2. Arm toward top of net
3. Move onto court

d   1

Detecting Underhand Serve Errors

Most underhand serve errors can be attributed to the position of the holding hand. Many beginning players swing the holding hand or hold the ball at a level higher than the waist. If you initially hold and maintain the ball at the correct location, you should have relatively high success at performing this serve.

ERROR

CORRECTION

1. The ball goes up more than forward and does not travel over the net.

1. Hold the ball at waist level or lower. Contact the ball just below center back and swing arm forward toward the net. Transfer your weight onto your forward foot.

2. The ball does not have enough force to make it over the net.

2. Do not swing holding hand; hit a stationary ball. Contact must be made with the heel of your open hand.

ERROR

CORRECTION

3. Your weight ends up on your back foot; the ball trajectory is too high.

3. Step forward onto your front foot as you contact the ball.

Underhand Serve
Keys to Success Checklist

When checking for performance errors of the underhand serve, you need to look for three problems that tend to be the basis of all such errors: (a) you fail to transfer your weight from your back foot to your forward foot, (b) you hold the ball too high or move it away from your body as you serve, and (c) you swing your hitting arm toward the ceiling instead of toward the top of the net. These problems are somewhat related because a transfer of weight backward usually causes your holding arm to rise and your hitting arm to swing toward the ceiling. As an instructor or other skilled player reviews this checklist, he or she should watch for these three basic problems.

Preparation Phase

____ Feet are in a staggered, comfortable stride position.
____ Weight is evenly distributed.
____ Ball is held at waist height or lower, to the center from front foot.
____ Shoulders are square to the net.
____ Eyes are on the ball.

Execution Phase

____ Server swings arm back and transfers weight to rear foot.
____ Arm swings forward and weight transfers to front foot as ball is contacted.
____ Server contacts ball with heel of open hand at waist level as ball-holding hand drops.
____ Holding hand does not swing forward.
____ Eyes stay on ball until contact.

Follow-Through Phase

____ Hand swings forward toward the top of the net.
____ Weight ends up on front foot.
____ Server moves onto court to defensive position.

HOW TO EXECUTE THE OVERHAND FLOATER SERVE

The essential element in executing the floater serve is the toss. The toss must be just in front of your hitting shoulder at a height that allows you time to swing your arm and still contact the ball at full extension. The toss must be made with little or no spin on the ball. Stand with a slight stride position, shoulders square to the net, foot of your noncontact side forward, and your weight evenly distributed. As you toss the ball, bring your hitting arm back with the elbow high and hand close to your ear. As your arm swings forward toward the ball, keep your eyes on the ball. Make contact with the heel of your open hand slightly below the center back of the ball. The ball contact is a poking action with no follow-through. As your arm swings through the ball, your weight is transferred to your front foot. Continue forward to assume a defensive position. The key to consistent serving is the elimination of all extraneous movements, for example, extra steps and unnecessary or tennislike follow-throughs (see Figure 3.2).

Figure 3.2 Keys to Success: ***Overhand Floater Serve***

Preparation Phase

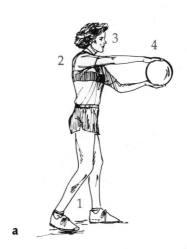

1. Stride position
2. Shoulders square to net
3. Eyes on ball
4. Open hitting hand

Execution
Phase

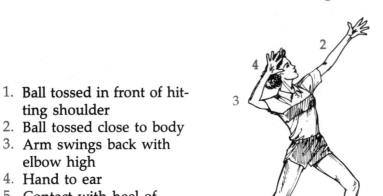

1. Ball tossed in front of hitting shoulder
2. Ball tossed close to body
3. Arm swings back with
   elbow high
4. Hand to ear
5. Contact with heel of
   open hand
6. Contact at full extension
7. Poking action

Follow-Through
Phase

1. Weight on front foot
2. No follow-through of
   arm
3. Move onto court

Detecting Overhand Floater Serve Errors

Most overhand floater serve errors are due to bad tosses. Good placement of the ball on the toss is essential to success. Much time can be saved if you practice the toss by itself until you are proficient at it. Practice serving against a wall until your form is consistent. You should execute the serve with exactly the same form every time, changing only the angle of your body to change the direction of the ball.

ERROR

CORRECTION

1. The ball goes into the net.

2. The serve goes off to the right. (Note: this is true for both right and left-handed players.)

1. Be sure toss is close to the shoulder of your hitting hand.

2. The toss must be in front of your body and not to the right side of your body.

ERROR   **CORRECTION**

3. The serve lacks the power to reach the net.

3. Use your entire body when you serve; contact the ball with the heel of your hand, not just the fingers.

4. The ball goes over the end line of your opponent's court.

4. Make contact just below the ball's center back; make sure you contact the ball in front of your body.

5. You have to take steps to get to a toss that is too far out in front.

5. Check for toss accuracy; the toss must be close to your body, just in front of your hitting shoulder.

Overhand Floater Serve
Keys to Success Checklist

When checking your overhand floater serve, the best position for your instructor is directly behind you. From this position it is easier to evaluate tossing proficiency (using the checklist below). Servers often toss the ball to the outside of their hitting shoulders; this error is not easily observed by someone standing to the side of the server.

**Preparation
Phase**

____ Feet are in a comfortable stride position.
____ Weight is evenly distributed.
____ Shoulders are square to the net.
____ Noncontact side foot is forward.
____ Eyes are on the ball.

**Execution
Phase**

____ Ball is tossed in front of the hitting shoulder with little or no spin.
____ Ball is tossed with one hand.
____ Hitting arm swings back with elbow high and hand close to the ear.
____ Ball is contacted with the heel of open hand at full extension.
____ Eyes are on ball until contact.
____ Weight transfers onto forward foot at contact.

Follow-Through Phase

_____ Weight is on front foot.
_____ There is no follow-through of the arm.
_____ Server moves onto the court.

Serving Drills

1. Ball Toss Drill

Place a 12-inch–square target on the floor in front and slightly to the center from your forward foot. Stand in serving position and hold your hitting hand fully extended. Toss the ball so that it goes higher than your hitting hand and lands on the target.

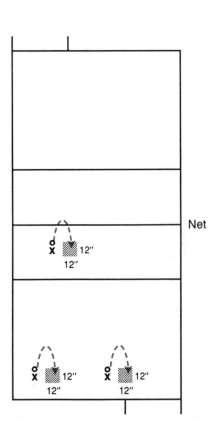

Success Goal = 9 accurate tosses out of 10 attempts

Your Score = (#) _____ tosses

2. *Wall Serve Drill*

Stand in a serving position approximately 20 feet from a wall on which is painted a line at the proper net height. Toss and serve the ball into the wall above the line.

Success Goal = a. 9 good underhand serves out of 10 attempts
b. 9 good overhand floater serves out of 10 attempts

Your Score = a. (#) _____ underhand serves
b. (#) _____ overhand floater serves

3. *Partner Serve at the Net Drill*

You and a partner should stand in opposite sides of the court, each 20 feet from the net. Serve the ball cleanly over the net (the ball not touching the net) to your partner. Your partner must be able to catch the ball without moving more than one step in any direction.

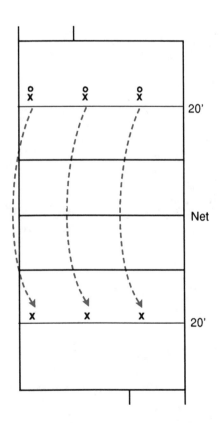

Success Goal = a. 7 out of 10 accurate underhand serves
b. 7 out of 10 accurate overhand floater serves

Your Score = a. (#) _____ underhand serves
b. (#) _____ overhand floater serves

4. *End Line Serve Drill*

You and a partner should stand on opposite end lines. Serve cleanly back and forth to each other's side of the court.

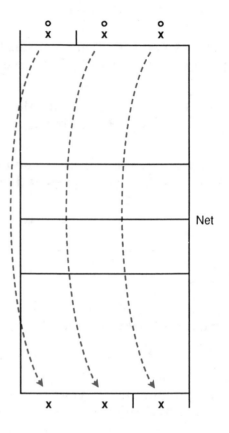

Success Goal = a. 9 out of 10 good underhand serves
b. 9 out of 10 good overhand floater serves

Your Score = a. (#) ____ underhand serves
b. (#) ____ overhand floater serves

5. *Consistency Drill*

This is the same as the previous drill, but with different Success Goals.

Success Goal = a. 25 consecutive good underhand serves
b. 25 consecutive good overhand floater serves

Your Score = a. (#) ____ consecutive underhand serves
b. (#) ____ consecutive overhand floater serves

6. Serve for Accuracy Drill

Place a sheet approximately 10 feet square in one of the six rotational positions on one side of the court. Stand in the opposite serving area (the right third of the court) and serve, attempting to hit the target. You should attempt this drill for all six target areas.

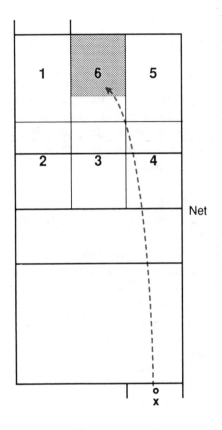

Success Goal = a. 20 or fewer underhand serves needed to hit a target 5 times, repeating for each target

b. 20 or fewer overhand floater serves needed to hit a target 5 times, repeating for each target

Your Score = a. (#) _____ underhand serves, target 1
(#) _____ underhand serves, target 2
(#) _____ underhand serves, target 3
(#) _____ underhand serves, target 4
(#) _____ underhand serves, target 5
(#) _____ underhand serves, target 6
b. (#) _____ overhand floater serves, target 1
(#) _____ overhand floater serves, target 2
(#) _____ overhand floater serves, target 3
(#) _____ overhand floater serves, target 4
(#) _____ overhand floater serves, target 5
(#) _____ overhand floater serves, target 6

7. Call and Serve Drill

Each side of the volleyball court is divided into six equal areas, three by the end line, three along the net. These areas are numbered counterclockwise, beginning with *1* in the right back position. Short (net) areas are numbered *2*, *3*, and *4*, and long areas are *5*, *6*, and *1*.

Indicate which area you are serving to by calling out the number of this area prior to serving. Points are awarded as follows: 3 points for hitting the target called, 2 points if the target is missed but the serve hits an adjacent target at the same distance (both short or both long), and 1 point for a serve at the opposite distance.

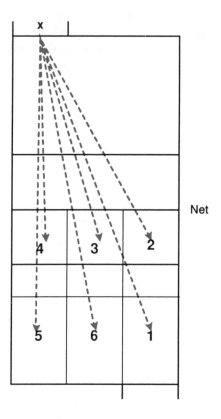

Success Goal = a. 20 points on 10 underhand serves
b. 20 points on 10 overhand floater serves

Your Score = a. (#) _____ points on 10 underhand serves
b (#) _____ points on 10 overhand floater serves

Step 4   Two-Skill Combination

By this point, you have learned movement patterns in volleyball and the skills of forearm passing and serving. You are now ready to combine these skills as they would be used in a game situation.

WHY IS THIS TWO-SKILL COMBINATION IMPORTANT?

The typical serve comes to the receiver with a good deal of force. Even though the rules do not stipulate that the serve must be received by using a forearm pass, volleyball officials currently accept only this method of playing the serve.

The reception of serve is the starting point of your team's attempt to gain a side out. Therefore, it is extremely important that serve reception is successful. A quality of serve reception essential for success is your ability to anticipate the direction of the ball, to determine whether you are the one who is going to receive it. The sooner you determine that you will receive the serve, the more time you have to get into the correct position. You must call for the ball by yelling ''I have it'' or ''mine.'' This call should be made before the ball crosses the net and arrives in your court.

The best means of predicting the direction of the opponent's serve is to concentrate on the server's body. You should look for the angle of the server's shoulders, where the forward foot is pointing, and the direction of the hitting arm. The sooner that you can determine the serve direction, the better your chance of executing a good pass. It is even possible for you to cover the entire court by yourself and touch every serve if you pay attention to the server's body cues.

Two-Skill Combination Drills

1. Simulated Serve and Pass Drill

In a group of three players with two balls, the tosser is on one side of the net at the attack line. You and the other player are on the opposite side of the net. You are the receiver, standing in the backcourt midway between the attack line and the end line. The other is a target player, standing near the net to your right.

The tosser, using a two-hand method, throws one ball over the net toward you. Call for the ball and forearm pass it higher than (not over) the net to the target, who should not have to move more than one step in any direction. Meanwhile, the target has delivered the second ball to the tosser. The tosser immediately tosses the second ball, then receives and tosses the first ball, and so on, making the drill continuous.

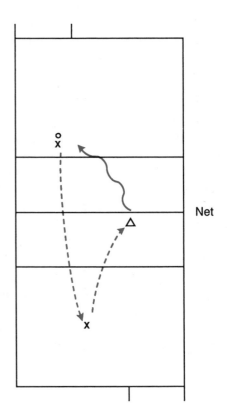

Net

Success Goal = 20 accurate forearm passes out of 25 attempts

Your Score = (#) _____ forearm passes

2. *Serve and Forearm Pass Drill*

You are the receiver in a group of three players in the same basic formation as the previous drill. Now, though, the tosser moves to the service area and serves the ball with an underhand serve. You call for the ball and forearm pass it with proper height and accuracy to the target player, who returns it to the server. When you switch positions, pay close attention to your service techniques.

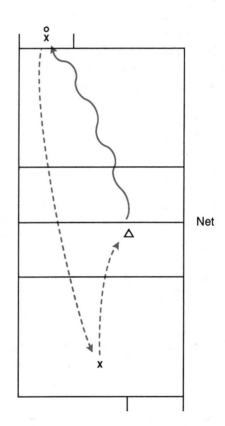

Net

Success Goal = a. 15 out of 25 good forearm passes

b. 25 out of 30 legal underhand serves

c. 25 out of 30 legal overhand floater serves

Your Score = a. (#) _____ forearm passes

b. (#) _____ underhand serves

c. (#) _____ overhand floater serves

3. Serve and Forearm Pass for Accuracy From Right Back Position Drill

This is the same as the previous drill except that now when you're the passer, stand in the right back position, call for the ball, and pass the ball so that the ball is higher than the net and falls to the court in a 10-foot-square target. This target is bounded by the centerline and the attack line, and begins 5 feet from the right sideline. The target person catches the ball after it bounces, then returns it to the server. When it's your turn to serve, be sure to serve to the half of the opposite court where the receiver is standing.

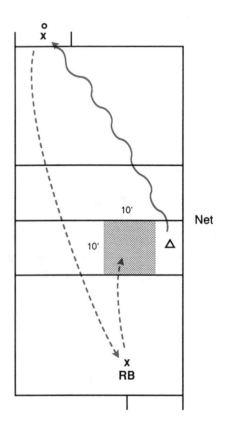

Success Goal = a. 6 out of 10 good forearm pass attempts
   b. 10 out of 12 legal underhand serves
   c. 10 out of 12 legal overhand floater serves

Your Score = a. (#) _____ forearm passes
   b. (#) _____ underhand serves
   c. (#) _____ overhand floater serves

4. *Serve and Forearm Pass for Accuracy From Left Back Position Drill*

This is the same as the previous drill, with the exception that the receiver is in the left back position.

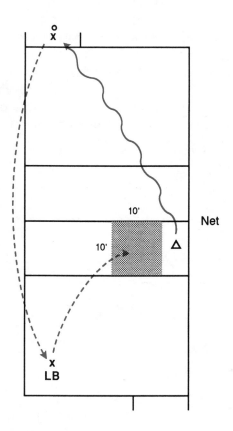

Success Goal = a. 6 out of 10 good forearm pass attempts
  b. 10 out of 12 legal underhand serves
  c. 10 out of 12 legal overhand floater serves

Your Score = a. (#) ____ forearm passes
  b. (#) ____ underhand serves
  c. (#) ____ overhand floater serves

5. *Calling the Pass Drill*

In a group of four, two of you be receivers in the left back and right back positions, one be a target person in the right third of the court near the net, and the fourth be a server on the opposite side of the net.

   The server should vary the serves and hit them into each of the three deep positions. One or the other of the receivers should call for each serve and pass it to the target as in previous drills.

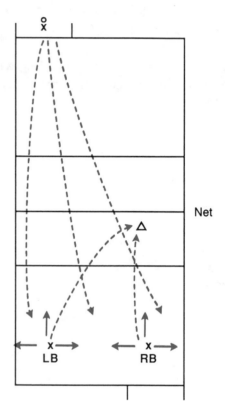

Success Goal = a. 6 out of 10 good forearm pass attempts
             b. 10 out of 12 legal underhand serves into each of the three deep positions
             c. 10 out of 12 legal overhand floater serves into each of the three deep positions

Your Score = a. (#) _____ forearm passes
             b. (#) _____ underhand serves into each of the three deep positions
             c. (#) _____ overhand floater serves into each of the three deep positions

Step 5 Overhead Pass

The next skill for you to learn is the overhead pass. This skill should be the one in which you handle the ball with the greatest efficiency and the most control. You use the overhead pass to move the ball to a teammate and, rarely, to return the ball to the opponents. This pass is executed primarily by the setter in order to deliver the ball to the attacker, but it may be used by any player to accomplish this task. You should be able to execute this skill either forward or backward without changing the style of delivery.

WHY IS THE OVERHEAD PASS IMPORTANT?

The overhead pass is usually your team's second contact of the ball in the three-step offensive effort. In most offensive situations, one player is designated as the setter and is the player who executes the second hit, or *set*. This person should be the best overhead passer on the team.

The overhead pass can be used by a player receiving any ball higher than shoulder level and coming to the player with little force. You should use the overhead pass whenever appropriate. Do not let the ball drop to forearm pass level, because the overhead pass is the most efficient way to handle the ball.

HOW TO EXECUTE THE OVERHEAD PASS

The ready position is a slight stride, your feet shoulder-width apart, your knees bent, and your hands raised in front of your forehead at a distance of approximately 6–8 inches, your thumbs pointing toward your eyes. Form a "window" with your thumbs and pointer fingers in such a manner that your fingers are twice as far apart as your thumbs. Watch the ball through this window. It is extremely important that your shoulders be positioned squarely toward the target. As the ball contacts your hands, your hands form to the shape of the ball with only the upper two joints of your fingers and thumbs actually touching the ball. As the ball contacts your fingers, extend your arms and legs, transferring your weight in the intended direction of the pass (see Figure 5.1).

Figure 5.1 Keys to Success: Overhead Pass

Preparation Phase

1. Stride position
2. Knees and hips slightly bent
3. Shoulders square to target
4. Hands in front of forehead
5. Form "window"
6. Look through window at ball

Execution Phase

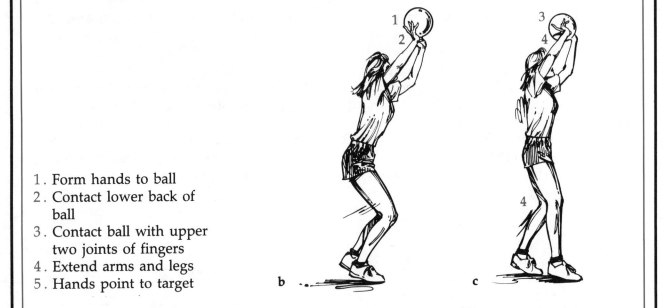

1. Form hands to ball
2. Contact lower back of ball
3. Contact ball with upper two joints of fingers
4. Extend arms and legs
5. Hands point to target

**Follow-Through
Phase**

1. Hands and arms extend
   to target
2. Transfer weight toward
   target
3. Move in direction of ball

Detecting Overhead Pass Errors

Most players have difficulty performing the overhead pass for two major reasons. First, such a player does not take position behind the ball with the shoulders square to the intended target. Second, the player attempts to play the ball from a body position in which the arms and legs are already fully extended. You are encouraged to move to the correct court position, then wait in a medium body posture for the ball to come down to you.

ERROR

CORRECTION

1. The ball contacts your palms and is "held."

1. Spread your fingers, wrap them around the ball, and contact the ball with only the upper two joints of your fingers and thumbs.

2. The ball travels vertically, instead of high and toward the target.

2. Your limb extension and weight transfer should be forward toward the target. Contact the ball at its lower back, not its bottom.

ERROR ⊘

3. You have difficulty directing the ball toward the target.

4. The ball spins excessively.

⊘

CORRECTION

3. Your shoulders *must* be positioned squarely toward the target. Equal force should be imparted to the ball with each of your hands.

4. You must give the ball immediate impetus; do not roll it off your hands.

Overhead Pass Drills

1. Pass-Bounce-Pass Drill

Overhead pass the ball at least 5 feet into the air, let it drop to the floor, and pass the ball again as it rises from the floor. Keep the ball in an area the size of half of one side of the court.

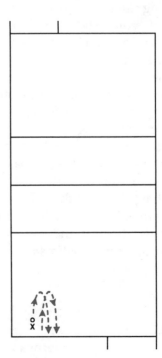

Success Goal = 25 consecutive overhead passes

Your Score = (#) _____ overhead passes

2. *Partner Toss and Pass Drill*

Have a partner toss a volleyball high and easy toward you. Overhead pass the ball back so that your partner can catch it without moving more than one step in any direction.

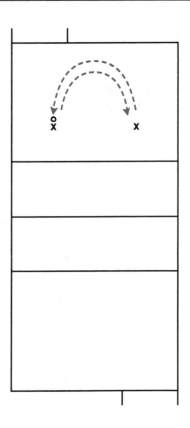

Success Goal = 8 good overhead passes to your partner

Your Score = (#) _____ overhead passes

3. *Free Ball Passing Drill*

In a group of three players, have one be the tosser, standing on one side of the net near the attack line. You be the receiver, standing on the other side in a blocking position at the net (standing close to the net, your hands held in front of your shoulders, your fingers spread). The third player stands at the attack line as the setter.

The tosser yells "free" and then tosses the ball over the net high and to the attack line. You, the receiver, move off the net to the attack line when hearing "free." Pass the ball overhead to the setter, who has moved to the net on the "free" signal. Your passes should be 2–3 feet higher than the net; the setter shouldn't have to adjust the net position taken by more than one step to field your pass. The setter catches the ball and returns it to the tosser. You all return to your starting positions and practice more.

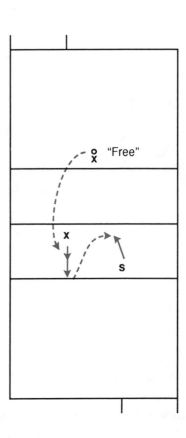

Success Goal = 8 out of 10 good overhead passes

Your Score = (#) _____ overhead passes

4. *Short Pass, Back Pass, Long Pass Drill*

In a group of three, stand in a line approximately 10 feet apart, two players facing in one direction and the third player facing them. The player facing the other two players initiates the drill with an ovehead pass to the middle player, who back sets the ball to the third player, who then long passes the ball back to the starting player.

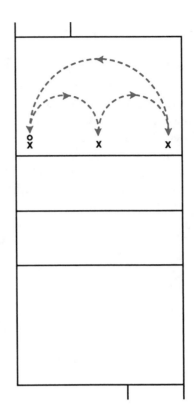

Success Goal = 15 consecutive 3-pass sequences

Your Score = (#) _____ 3-pass sequences

5. *Pass, Move, Pass Drill*

Start this drill facing a partner. Player A overhead passes to player B and runs to a position behind player B. Player B receives the pass, overhead passes the ball to him- or herself, back passes to player A, and turns to face player A. Player A receives the pass and, keeping the ball moving, overhead passes the ball back to player B, starting the sequence over. This drill can continue indefinitely.

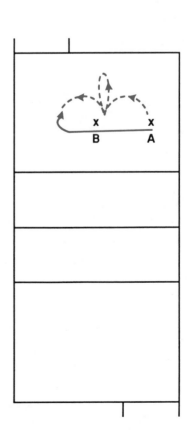

Success Goal = 10 consecutive front-back
                   pass sequences

Your Score = (#) _____ front-back pass sequences

6. *Pass Around and Back Drill*

Facing a partner as in the previous drill, player A overhead passes the ball to player B. This time, though, player A runs all the way around player B and back to the starting position. Player B, meanwhile, overhead passes the ball to him- or herself while A is circumnavigating B. When A gets back to the starting position, B overhead passes back to A. Keeping the ball moving, A starts the sequence over.

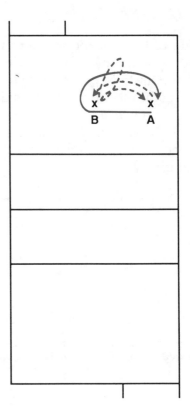

Success Goal = 10 consecutive pass-and-go sequences

Your Score = (#) _____ pass-and-go sequences

Overhead Pass
Keys to Success Checklist

The overhead pass is a very important volleyball skill. You should feel confident in your ability to handle any high, easy ball successfully by using the overhead pass. Beginning players need to realize that the force imparted to the ball during execution uses the total body, especially when the pass needs to cover a large distance. You apply this force to the ball by extending your arms and legs, and transferring your weight forward.

Have an instructor or another skilled volleyball player check your technique with the following list.

Preparation Phase

_____ Feet are in a comfortable stride position.
_____ Body moves to the ball.
_____ Arms and legs are slightly bent.
_____ Hands are held 6–8 inches above forehead.
_____ Eyes follow ball through the ''window'' formed by the fingers and thumbs.

Execution Phase

_____ Fingers and thumbs contact ball.
_____ Ball is contacted on its lower back.
_____ Arms and legs extend toward the target.
_____ Weight transfers toward the target.

Follow-Through
Phase

_____ Arms are fully extended, with hands pointing toward the target.
_____ Player moves in the direction of the pass.

Step 6 Set

The set is an overhead pass that you execute to place the ball in a position for the attack. The set can either be a forward pass or a back pass. The height of the set depends upon the type of spike desired.

WHY IS THE SET IMPORTANT?

The set determines where and how well the attack develops. Generally, a team designates one or two players to perform the setting duties. It is extremely important that these players have outstanding ability in setting the ball efficiently. A well-placed set enhances the attacking team's ability to gain an advantage over the opponent.

HOW TO EXECUTE THE SET

The setter takes a position on the right side of the court, close to the net and facing the left sideline. The set is executed in the same manner as the overhead pass. The overhead pass is called a *set* only when it is the second pass by your team and is used to direct the attack. When you set the ball to an attacker, it should be at least a foot off (back away from) the net so that the attacker can hit the ball hard without contacting the net (see Figure 6.1).

Sets in volleyball are usually identified by a numbering system combining two digits. One digit indicates the height of the set above the net; the second digit indicates the spot,

either on the net or in relationship to the setter, where the ball will be directed. Teams can develop play-calling systems that are quite complicated. The United States National teams are currently utilizing a three-digit system, the third digit indicating the set's distance from the net.

For the purpose of this introductory book, it will do to discuss three basic sets: the high outside, the quick, and the back set. The *high outside set* is placed on the left side of the court so that, if left alone, it would drop on the left sideline. It is set at least 6 feet higher than the top of the net. In the high set, it is the attacker's responsibility to go to the ball.

The *quick set* is always set in relation to the setter. The setter sets the ball directly in front of himself or herself and 1–2 feet higher than the top of the net. In a quick set, it is the setter's responsibility to set the ball accurately to the attacker. The attacker approaches in front of the setter and jumps as or before the setter contacts the ball.

The *back set* needs less traveling distance than the high outside set and requires less height (5–6 feet higher than the top of the net). The back set is performed with the same technique as the front set except that as the setter contacts the ball, the back is arched and the ball is directed toward the ceiling. A good setter prepares to execute all sets exactly the same way so as not to give the opponents any indication of the intended set (Figure 6.2).

Figure 6.1   Keys to Success: *The Set*

Preparation Phase

1. Stride position
2. Knees and hips slightly bent
3. Shoulders square to target
4. Hands in front of forehead
5. Form "window"
6. Look through window at ball

Execution Phase

1. Form hands to ball
2. Contact lower back of ball
3. Contact ball with upper two joints of fingers
4. Extend arms and legs
5. Hands point toward target

**Follow-Through
Phase**

1. Hands and arms extend
   to target
2. Transfer weight toward
   target
3. Move in direction of ball

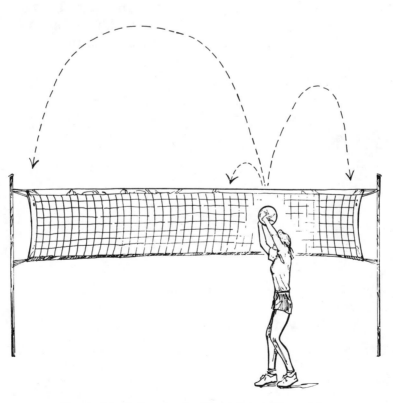

Figure 6.2 Ball paths for the high outside, quick,
and back sets.

Detecting Setting Errors

Your body position in relation to the net is a critical aspect of good setting. If you keep your right foot forward in the stride position, the set is less likely to cross over the net. You should always try to square your shoulders in the direction of the set before contacting the ball. This means that you will always set straight back or forward. When setting high outside, you have full view of the net and the attacker with this position.

ERROR

CORRECTION

1. The ball contacts the palms and is "held."

1. Spread your fingers, wrap them around the ball, and contact the ball only with the upper two joints of your fingers and thumbs.

ERROR   **CORRECTION**

2. The ball travels vertically, instead of high and toward the target.

2. Your extension and weight transfer should be forward toward the target. Contact the ball at its lower back, not at its bottom.

3. You have difficulty directing the ball toward the target.

4. The ball spins excessively.

3. Your shoulders *must* be positioned squarely toward the target.

4. You must give the ball immediate impetus; it must not roll off your hands.

ERROR   **CORRECTION**

5. The set crosses the net into the opponent's court.

6. The ball travels into the net.

7. The ball does not reach the sideline.

8. You set the ball too low.

5. When in position at the right front of the court, you should face the left sideline and have your right foot forward.

6. When you are in position to set, your shoulders should be squarely facing the intended target.

7. You must place the ball so that it will drop on the sideline.

8. The highest point of the set's trajectory should be 7–8 feet above the top of the net for the forward set, 5–6 feet for the back set.

Setting Drills

1. High Outside Set Drill

With a partner on a regulation court, stand 5 feet in from the right sideline, your partner standing just outside the left sideline.

Your partner begins the drill by tossing you the ball. You must set the ball to a height of at least 7 feet above the top of the net, and it should land within 1 foot of the left sideline.

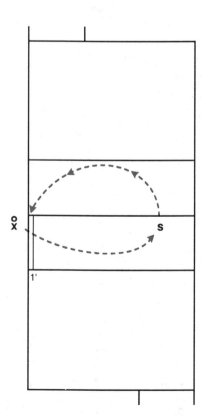

Success Goal = 15 out of 20 good sets

Your Score = (#) _____ sets

2. High Back Set Drill

For this drill you need two partners. One tosses a high ball to you, the setter, as you stand 5 feet in from the right sideline, as in the previous drill. Your other partner is positioned behind you, standing just outside the right sideline. You must back set the ball to a height of at least 5 feet above the top of the net, and it must land within one foot of the right sideline.

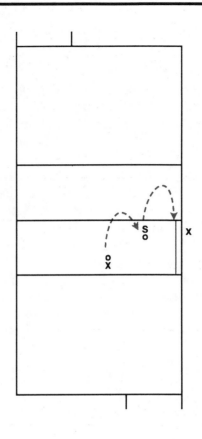

Success Goal = 15 out of 20 good sets

Your Score = (#) _____ sets

3. Quick Set Drill

With a partner, one of you be an attacker, the other a setter. The attacker begins at the attack line; the setter stands close to the net.

The attacker overhead passes the ball to the setter and quickly runs to the net. The setter quick sets the ball 1 foot in front of him- or herself and 1–2 feet higher than the top of the net. The attacker jumps just before or as the setter contacts the ball, raising the hitting hand as a target for the set. The attacker catches the ball, lands on both feet, and returns to the attack line. After several practice attempts, switch places.

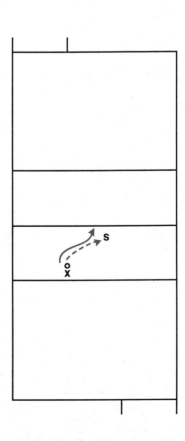

Success Goal = attacker and setter completing 5 out of 10 set attempts

Your Score = (#) _____ sets caught by the attacker

4. *Setting a Bad Pass Drill*

In a group of three players, one of you be the tosser, another the setter and the other a target player. The tosser stands in the backcourt; the setter begins in the right back position; the target stands on the left sideline 1–2 feet off the net.

The tosser calls "go" and tosses the ball high and at least 10 feet away from the net, simulating an inaccurate pass. The setter has run to the setting position at the net on the signal "go." The setter reacts to the toss, moves off the net, squares the shoulders to the left side of the court, and sets high outside to the target person. The set should be at least 7 feet higher than the net, and the target should not have to take more than one step to catch it.

Success Goal = 8 out of 10 high, outside sets caught

Your Score = (#) _____ high outside sets caught

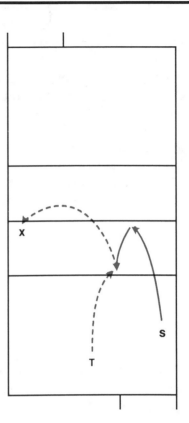

Setting
Keys to Success Checklist

It is often stated that an excellent setter can make an average attacker look good and an excellent attacker can make an average setter look good. It is essential that you be able to set the ball to the desired attack area regardless of the position of the pass. (As a setter, your job is facilitated by excellent passing, though.) You must have a strong desire to set every ball well; use the forearm pass skill to set only as a last resort.

Have a skillful observer check your setting abilities with this checklist.

Preparation Phase

_____ Feet are in a comfortable stagger stride with the right foot forward.
_____ Body moves to the ball and establishes position with the shoulders square to the target.
_____ Arms and legs are slightly bent.
_____ Hands are held 6–8 inches above forehead.
_____ Eyes follow ball through the ''window'' formed by the fingers and thumbs.

Execution Phase

_____ Ball is contacted with the fingers and thumbs.
_____ Arms and legs extend toward the target.
_____ Weight transfers toward the target.
_____ Ball is contacted on its lower back.
_____ Ball is at least 6 feet above the net for the front set, 5 feet above the net for the back set, and 1 foot above the net for the quick set.
_____ High front set drops to the left sideline, high back set drops to the right sideline; quick set is placed to the attacker's hitting hand.

**Follow-Through
Phase**

_____ Arms are fully extended with hands pointing toward the target.
_____ Player moves in the direction of the set.

Step 7 Three-Skill Combination

The ultimate goal of a volleyball team on offense is to complete the three-hit sequence of forearm pass, set, and attack. We are now ready to combine two of these skills with receiving the serve.

WHY IS THIS THREE-SKILL COMBINATION IMPORTANT?

Your team must convert a hard-driven serve coming to you into a ball that is easily manage-able. This requires cushioning the ball as you receive it and directing it high and easy to the setter. The setter must then place the ball in a position where the attacker can hit it aggressively back to the opponents. In order for this three-hit combination to be successful, all three components must be executed efficiently.

Three-Skill Combination Drills

1. Serve, Forearm Pass, and Set Drill

Assemble a group of four: a receiver in the left back position; a setter in the front at the net, at least 5 feet in from the right sideline; a target person just outside the left sideline; and, in the opposite court, a server in the service area.

The server makes an underhand serve to the left back of the other side. The receiver forearm passes the ball to the setter, who should not have to move more than a step to play the ball. The setter sets the ball high outside, at least 6 feet higher than the top of the net and landing within a foot of the left sideline. The target person lets the ball bounce to check its accuracy, then returns it to the server.

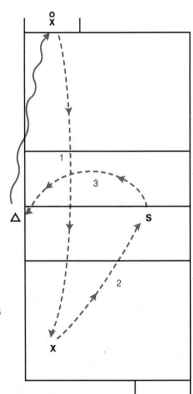

Success Goal = a. 12 out of 15 legal serves
b. 10 out of 12 good forearm passes
c. 8 out of 10 good sets

Your Score = a. (#) _____ serves
b. (#) _____ forearm passes
c. (#) _____ sets

2. Serve, Forearm Pass, and Back Set Drill

This is the same as the previous drill, except that the receiver takes the serve in the right back position, and the setter back sets the ball at least 5 feet higher than the net to within 1 foot of the right sideline.

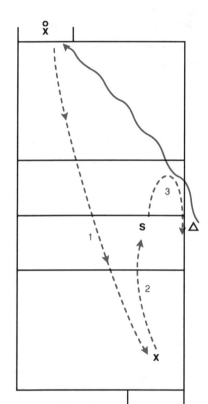

Success Goal = a. 12 out of 15 legal serves
b. 10 out of 12 good forearm passes
c. 8 out of 10 good back sets

Your Score = a. (#) _____ serves
b. (#) _____ forearm passes
c. (#) _____ back sets

3. Reception Decision Drill

In a group of five, have a server in the service area of the court and, on the opposite side, two receivers in the back left and right halves, a setter in the front of the court at the net at least 5 feet in from the right sideline, and a target person standing just outside the left sideline.

The ball is served underhand alternately to each back quarter of the court. The receivers determine who will play the ball and call for it prior to its crossing the net. The ball is forearm passed to the setter, who, as always, shouldn't have to move more than a step. The setter sets the ball high outside, at least 6 feet higher than the net and within 1 foot of the left sideline. The target person returns the ball to the server after letting it bounce.

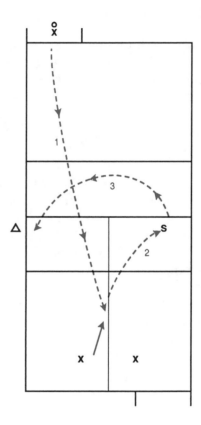

Success Goal = a. 6 out of 10 legal serves to each back quarter of the court
b. 5 out of 6 good forearm passes by each receiver
c. 8 out of 10 good sets

Your Score = a. (#) _____ serves
b. (#) _____ forearm passes
c. (#) _____ sets

4. Serve, Pass, and Set Game Drill

Two groups of four players each compete against each other in this drill. Each team has its server on one side of the net and its forearm passer, setter, and target person on the opposite side of the net.

Both teams hit the balls at the same time. A team scores 1 point each time they complete the combination of a legal serve, a good forearm pass, and a good set. A legal serve is a serve that crosses the net without touching it and lands within the boundaries of the court. A good pass is any pass that allows the setter to set without moving more than one step in any direction. A good set is a ball that goes at least 6 feet higher than the net and lands on or within 1 foot of the left sideline. The target person catches the set after it bounces and returns it to the serving teammate on the opposite side.

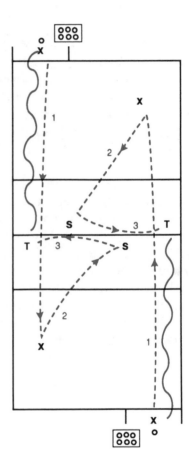

Success Goal = be the first team to make 20 points

Your Score = (#) _____ points

There are three methods of attack in volleyball, each of which can be very effective. The first to learn of the three methods is the *dink*. It is often looked upon as a defensive maneuver to be performed when the conditions are not right for a more powerful attack. However, the dink is also an extremely effective offensive technique used to disrupt the timing patterns of the defensive team.

The *off-speed spike* is a second option for the attacker. As indicated by its name, less than maximum force is imparted at contact. Like the dink, it is an extremely effective offensive technique used to disrupt the timing patterns of the defensive team.

A third attack method is the *hard-driven spike,* the most exciting play in volleyball. It is also one of the most difficult of all sports skills to learn. In order to make a successful spike, you must jump into the air and sharply hit a moving object (the ball) over an obstacle (the net) so that it lands within the bounded area (the court). Due to the many variables associated with spiking, its timing is difficult and its success requires hours of practice.

WHY IS THE ATTACK IMPORTANT?

When your opponents have mastered the timing of your attack, the dink can catch the opponents off-guard. It is much more difficult to cover the court defensively when a team effectively mixes the speed of their attack. A well-placed dink often "breaks the back" of the opposition and may help improve the momentum of the offense.

The attacking team attempts to have as many different options available to them as possible. The off-speed spike is similar in effect to the dink, but it is hit deeper into the opponent's court. When the off-speed spike is executed, placement is the emphasis, rather than power. The attacker hopes to force the defensive player to move from the starting defensive position and make an error in attempting to play the ball.

The hard-driven spike is the primary offensive weapon in volleyball. Most teams gain a majority of their points on successful spikes. The spike takes very little time to travel from the attacker's hand to the floor; therefore, there is little time for defensive players to move to the ball, and the defensive team must locate its players on the court in strategic positions before the ball is contacted on the spike. The hard-driven spike adds a great deal of excitement to the game and, thus, has tremendous spectator appeal.

HOW TO EXECUTE THE DINK

The approach to all three types of attack is the same. It is important because it increases the height of your jump and increases the force you are able to impart on the ball. For a high set, you, the attacker, begin on the attack line, wait for the set to be half the distance to you from the setter, and then move toward the set. Approach the net attempting to cover the distance with as few steps as possible. The last two steps are the most important. Make a two-footed takeoff by planting your right foot heel first and closing with your left foot (bringing the left foot to a position even with the right foot) or taking a hop onto both feet. As you plant both feet heels first to change forward momentum into upward momentum, swing your arms to prepare for a jump. Swing forward both arms and reach high toward the set as you jump straight up into the air. Draw your hitting arm back, your elbow high and your hand close to your ear. As you swing at the ball, your nonhitting hand drops quickly to your waist. Gently contact the ball by using the upper two joints of the fingers of your hitting hand, slightly in front of your hitting shoulder at full arm extension. Contact the ball slightly below the center back. Direct the ball upward enough to barely clear the block but still drop quickly to the floor. Return to the floor with a two-footed landing (see Figure 8.1).

Figure 8.1 Keys to Success: *Dink*

Preparation Phase

1. Wait on attack line
2. Watch setter
3. Eyes on ball after set
4. Weight forward
5. Anticipate approach to the net

Execution Phase

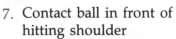

1. Begin approach to net when ball is at peak of its trajectory
2. Cover distance with few steps
3. Last two steps right, close left or step to jump

4. Arms swing back to waist level
5. Both arms swing forward
6. Both arms swing high toward ball

7. Contact ball in front of hitting shoulder
8. Contact with upper two joints of fingers
9. Contact on lower back half of ball
10. Contact with full arm extension

**Follow-Through
Phase**

1. Hand follows ball to target
2. Land on both feet
3. Bend knees to cushion landing

Detecting Dink Errors

Most dink errors are associated with improper hand position in relation to the ball and poor timing during the approach. Dinking success is closely associated to your ability to disguise the fact that you are going to dink. Up until hand contact, your approach should be exactly the same as that for a spike.

ERROR

CORRECTION

1. The ball goes into the net.

1. Contact the ball just in front of your hitting shoulder; the greater the distance the ball is in front of you, the lower it drops before contact and the greater the chance of its being hit into the net.

2. The ball does not clear the block.

2. Make contact on the back lower half of the ball and with your arm fully extended.

3. You stop your approach and wait for the ball.

3. You should not begin your approach until the ball is half the distance to you from the setter.

4. You contact the net.

4. The set must be at least 1 foot from the net; you must execute a heel plant to change horizontal momentum into vertical momentum.

5. You hit the ball too high, and it takes too long to hit the floor.

5. Contact the ball in front of your hitting shoulder.

Dink
Keys to Success Checklist

When performing the dink, keep in mind that your attack needs to go over or by the opponent's block in order to be successful. Your body must be behind the ball so you can direct the ball to the most advantageous area of the opponent's court. Also, be aware that officials will usually call you for improper technique if you attempt to change the direction of the ball during dink performance. This causes your hand to be in contact with the ball too long, which is a held ball.

Preparation Phase

_____ Weight is forward, attacker ready to move.

_____ Attacker remains at sideline until beginning approach.

_____ Attacker watches setter until ball is set, then focuses on the ball.

_____ Attacker waits at attack line until set is half the distance from the setter to the attacker.

Execution Phase

_____ Approach begins when set is half the distance from the setter to the attacker.

_____ Last two steps of approach are step right and close left or step to jump.

_____ Both arms swing back to waist height.

_____ Heels are planted to stop horizontal momentum.

_____ Weight transfers to balls of feet and arms swing forward and up.

_____ Ball is contacted with upper two joints of fingers.

_____ Ball is contacted with arm at full extension and in front of hitting shoulder.

_____ Ball is contacted on lower back half of the ball.

_____ Eyes on ball through contact.

**Follow-Through
Phase**

____ Hand follows through in direction of
dink and drops to the waist.
____ Attacker lands on two feet.
____ Bends knees on contact with floor to
absorb force.

HOW TO EXECUTE THE OFF-SPEED SPIKE

The execution of the off-speed spike is exactly
the same as that of the dink—until contact. In
the off-speed spike, hit the ball with the heel
of an open hand cutting into the center back
of the ball. At contact, your wrist snaps and
your fingers roll over the top of the ball, im-
parting topspin, which causes the ball to drop.
The follow-through is the same as for the dink
(see Figure 8.2).

Figure 8.2 Keys to Success: Off-Speed Spike

**Preparation
Phase**

1. Wait on attack line
2. Watch the setter
3. Eyes on ball after set
4. Weight forward
5. Anticipate approach

a

Execution
Phase

b   c   d

1. Begin approach when ball is at peak of its trajectory
2. Cover distance with few steps
3. Last two steps right and close left or step to jump
4. Arms swing back to waist level
5. Both arms swing forward

6. Both arms swing high toward ball
7. Contact ball in front of hitting shoulder
8. Contact with heel of open hand
9. Contact center back of ball
10. Fingers roll over top of ball
11. Wrist snaps
12. Contact with full arm extension

Follow-Through
Phase

1. Hand follows ball toward target
2. Land on both feet
3. Bend knees to cushion landing

Detecting Off-Speed Spike Errors

The off-speed spike is often referred to as a *roll shot*. This is because your hand rolls over the top of the ball as your wrist snaps. The hand action is important because it puts top-spin on the ball, causing the ball to drop quickly.

ERROR ⊘	CORRECTION
1. The ball goes into the net.	1. Contact the ball just in front of your hitting shoulder; the greater the distance the ball is in front of you, the lower it drops before contact and the greater the chance of its being hit into the net.
2. The ball does not clear the block.	2. Contact should be on the back lower half of the ball, with your arm fully extended; the fingers of your hand roll over top of the ball.
3. You stop approach and wait for the ball.	3. Do not begin the approach until the ball is half the distance to you from the setter.
4. You contact the net.	4. The set must be at least 1 foot from the net; you must execute a heel plant to change horizontal momentum into vertical momentum.
5. You hit the ball too high, and it takes too long to hit the floor.	5. Contact the ball in front of your hitting shoulder; your wrist must snap as your fingers roll over the top of the ball.

Off-Speed Spike Keys to Success Checklist

As previously indicated, the attack in volleyball is one of the most difficult skills in sport to perform. The most important element of good execution is proper timing. Beginners are often so anxious to complete the attack that they begin their approach much too early. You must watch the setter and follow the set to the highest point of its trajectory before initiating the approach.

Have your instructor or another skilled volleyball player use this checklist to evaluate your off-speed spike technique.

Preparation Phase

_____ Weight is forward, attacker ready to move.

_____ Attacker remains at sideline until beginning approach.

_____ Attacker watches setter until ball is set, then focuses on the ball.

_____ Attacker waits at attack line until set is half the distance from the setter to the attacker.

Execution Phase

_____ Approach begins when set is half the distance from the setter to attacker.

_____ Last two steps of approach are step right and close left or step to jump.

_____ Both arms swing back to waist height.

_____ Heels are planted to stop horizontal momentum.

_____ Weight transfers to balls of feet and arms swing forward and up.

_____ Ball is contacted with the heel of the hand.

_____ Fingers roll over the top of the ball.

_____ Ball is contacted with arm at full extension and in front of hitting shoulder.

_____ Ball is contacted on its lower back half.

_____ Eyes on ball throughout contact.

Follow-Through Phase

_____ Hand follows through in the direction of the spike and drops to the waist.
_____ Attacker lands on two feet.
_____ Bends knees on contact with floor.

HOW TO EXECUTE THE HARD-DRIVEN SPIKE

The execution of the hard-driven spike is the same as the execution of the off-speed spike until contact. In the hard-driven spike, contact the ball with the heel of an open hand cutting into the center back. At contact, your wrist snaps forcibly, and your arm drops forcibly toward your waist. The wrist snap imparts topspin, causing the ball to drop quickly to the floor. The follow-through is the same as for the off-speed spike (see Figure 8.3).

Figure 8.3   Keys to Success: *Hard-Driven Spike*

Preparation Phase

1. Wait on attack line
2. Watch the setter
3. Eyes on the ball after set
4. Weight forward
5. Anticipate approach

a

Execution
Phase

1. Begin approach when ball is at peak of its trajectory
2. Cover distance with few steps
3. Last two steps right and close left or step to jump
4. Arms swing back at least to waist level
5. Both arms swing forward
6. Both arms swing high toward ball
7. Contact ball in front of hitting shoulder
8. Contact with heel of open hand
9. Contact at center back
10. Use forcible wrist snap
11. Contact with full arm extension

**Follow-Through
Phase**

1. Hand follows ball
   toward target
2. Land on both feet
3. Bend knees to cushion
   landing

Detecting Hard-Driven Spike Errors

Two errors that are fairly common in executing the hard-driven spike are (a) beginning the approach too soon and (b) contacting the ball behind the hitting shoulder. If you approach the ball too soon, this is readily evident in two possible results: (a) you have to stop, wait for the set, and thus lose the benefit of the approach; or (b) you have to back up to attack the ball because you have approached to an incorrect position on the court. Balls contacted behind the hitting shoulder consistently go out-of-bounds.

ERROR   **CORRECTION**

1. The ball goes into the net.

1. Contact the ball just in front of the hitting shoulder; the greater the distance the ball is in front of you, the lower it drops before contact and the greater the chance of its being hit into the net.

2. You stop approach and wait for the ball.

2. You should not begin the approach until the ball is half the distance to you from the setter.

ERROR	CORRECTION

3. You contact the net.

3. The set must be at least 1 foot from the net; you must execute a heel plant to change horizontal momentum into vertical momentum.

4. The ball goes out-of-bounds over the end line.

4. You *must* contact the ball in front of your hitting shoulder; your wrist snaps your hand over the top of the ball.

5. You lack height on the jump.

5. You must plant your heels to convert horizontal momentum into vertical momentum; both arms must swing forcibly upward.

ERROR

CORRECTION

6. The set goes by you.

6. You must wait at the attack line until you know where the set will be.

Hard-Driven Spike
Keys to Success Checklist

For successful hard-driven spikes, you need to concentrate on three areas of performance: (a) timing of your approach, (b) keeping the ball in front of your hitting shoulder, and (c) a forcible wrist snap to impart topspin to the ball. Due to the complexity of the hard-driven spike, it is suggested that you practice parts of the skill individually prior to putting them together. For example, you can approach and jump without using a ball.

Have someone use this list to check your hard-driven spike.

Preparation
Phase

_____ Weight is forward, attacker ready to move.

_____ Attacker remains at sideline until beginning approach.

_____ Attacker watches setter until the ball is set, then focuses on the ball.

_____ Attacker waits at attack line until set is half the distance from the setter to the attacker.

Execution
Phase

_____ Approach begins when set is half the distance from the setter to attacker.

_____ Last two steps of approach are step right and close left or step to jump.

_____ Both arms swing back to waist height.

_____ Heels are planted to stop horizontal momentum.

_____ Weight transfers to balls of feet and arms swing forward and up.

_____ Ball is contacted with the heel of an open hand quickly followed by a snap of the wrist directing the hand over the top of the ball.

_____ Ball is contacted with arm at full extension and in front of hitting shoulder.

_____ Ball is contacted on its center back.

_____ Eyes on ball up to contact.

**Follow-Through
Phase**

_____ Hand follows through in the direction of the spike and drops to the waist.
_____ Attacker lands on two feet.
_____ Bend knees on contact with floor to absorb force.

Attack Drills

1. Dink to Target Drill

This drill requires a group of three players—you as attacker starting at the attack line, another at the net as the setter, and the other standing on a chair on the opposite side of the net as a blocker. A 5-foot wide target is located on the floor directly behind the blocker, from the centerline to the attack line. A second target, 10-feet wide, is between the centerline and the attack line, beginning 10 feet from the sideline.

The setter tosses the ball high to the outside of the court. You approach and dink over the blocker's hands, which are extended over the top of the net. During your practices as attacker, dink onto each target.

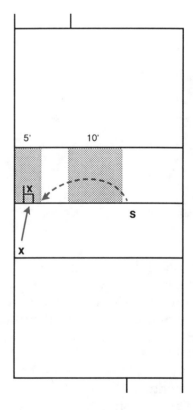

Success Goal = a. 5 dinks landing in the 5-foot wide target area out of 10 tosses
b. 5 dinks landing in the 10-foot wide target area out of 10 tosses

Your Score = a. (#) _____ dinks in 5-foot wide target
b. (#) _____ dinks in 10-foot wide target

2. *Off-Speed Spike to Center Court Drill*

This is almost the same as the previous drill. Your target here is a 10-foot square placed 5 feet from the net (extending 10 feet toward the end line). Place the target starting 10 feet in from each sideline.

As attacker, hit off-speed spikes over the blocker and onto the target from both the left and right sides of the court.

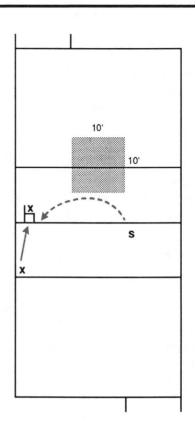

Success Goal = 10 out of 15 good off-speed spikes

Your Score = (#) _____ off-speed spikes

3. *Spike Hit Against Wall Drill*

Stand by yourself with a ball 10 feet away from a wall. Spike the ball into the floor. The ball should bounce sharply off the floor, rebound off the wall, and come back to you on the fly Spike the ball again and continuously.

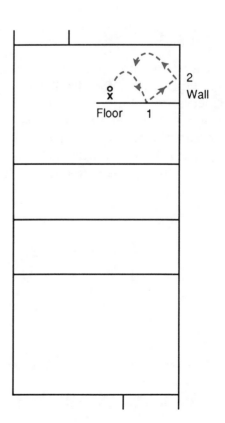

Success Goal = 25 consecutive sharp spike hits

Your Score = (#) _____ spike hits

4. Spike Hit for Direction Drill

With a partner, you begin as a spiker at the attack line near either sideline. Your partner is a setter near the net. Mark two 10-foot-square target areas in the back corners of the opponent's court.

Pass the ball high to your partner. Your partner sets the ball back to you. Without jumping, spike hit the ball over the net to either of the two large target areas.

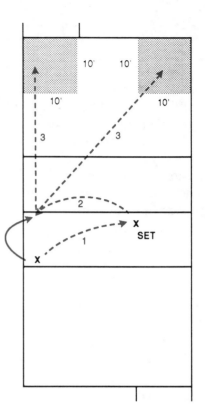

Success Goal = a. 5 out of 10 spike hits landing in the left back target area
b. 5 out of 10 spike hits landing in the right back target area

Your Score = a. (#) _____ spike hits landing on the left target
b. (#) _____ spike hits landing on the right target

5. Approach and Throw Drill

With a partner on the other side of the net, begin with a ball at the attack line. Approach the net carrying the ball, jump, and throw the ball forcibly over the net using a two-hand overhead motion with a wrist snap. Attempt to hit the front two-thirds of the court. Your partner retrieves the ball and rolls it back to you.

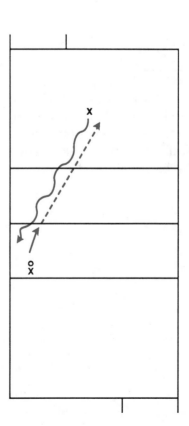

Success Goal = 10 out of 15 good tosses

Your Score = (#) _____ tosses

6. *Bounce and Spike Drill*

You and a partner set up as in the previous drill. Beginning at the attack line, bounce the ball forcibly into the floor, jump, and spike the rebound over the net. The ball must land within the boundaries of the opponent's court. Your partner retrieves the ball and rolls it back to you.

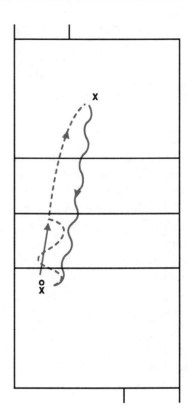

Success Goal = 10 good spikes out of 15 bounces

Your Score = (#) _____ spikes

7. *Spiking From a Set Drill*

In a group of four players, a tosser stands on one side of the net, and a passer, a setter, and an attacker set up on the opposite side.

The tosser throws the ball hard over the net to the receiver, who is standing in the backcourt. The receiver forearm passes the ball to the setter, who sets the ball high outside to the attacker, who spikes the ball over the net.

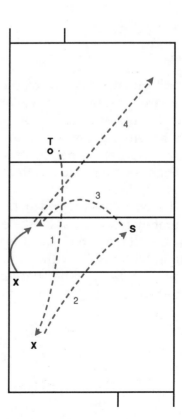

Success Goal = 8 out of 10 good spikes

Your Score = (#) _____ spikes

Step 9   Four-Skill Combination

Now that you have learned the attack, you are ready to complete the three-part sequence of forearm pass, set, and attack. The purpose of this sequence is to convert the opponent's attack or serve into your own attack. This conversion is referred to as a *transition*. After you receive your opponent's serve by cushioning it and passing it high to your setter, the setter places the ball in position for the attack. There are several types of sets, which are usually classified according to their placement and height. However, for the purposes of this first step—combining the three parts of the sequence—use only high, outside sets.

WHY IS THIS FOUR-SKILL COMBINATION IMPORTANT?

Your team must be able to receive your opponent's serve and quickly and efficiently change from defense to offense. If your team is unable to make this transition, you will be forced to return a free ball to your opponents. A *free ball* is any ball that is returned over the net in a manner other than an attack. A free ball is easy to receive by the opponents, who can quickly gain an advantage by making a perfect pass and completing the transition into their own attack. Teams that are continually forced to return free balls to their opponents find themselves constantly on defense.

Four-Skill Combination Drills

1. *Serve, Forearm Pass, Set, and Attack Drill*

For this drill, you need a group of four players. One serves from the service area of one side of the court. On the other side, you have a receiver in the left back position; a setter in the front of the court at the net, at least 5 feet in from the right sideline; and an attacker standing at the attack line.

The ball is served underhand to the receiver, who accurately forearm passes the ball to the setter. The setter sets the ball at least 6 feet higher than the net and within 1 foot of the sideline to the attacker. The attacker hits the ball over the net using any one of the three attacks.

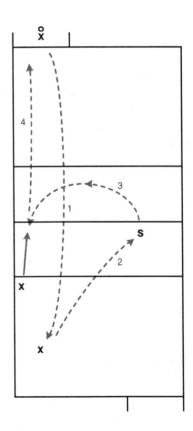

Success Goal = a. 12 out of 15 legal serves
                  b. 10 out of 12 accurate forearm passes
                  c. 8 out of 10 good sets
                  d. 5 out of 8 successful hits

Your Score = a. (#) _____ serves
               b. (#) _____ forearm passes
               c. (#) _____ sets
               d. (#) _____ attacks

2. Serve, Forearm Pass, Back Set, and Attack Drill

This is almost the same as the previous drill. Here, though, the serve goes to the receiver now in the right back quarter. Also, the setter back sets at least 5 feet higher than the net to the attacker, who is now at the attack line on the right sideline.

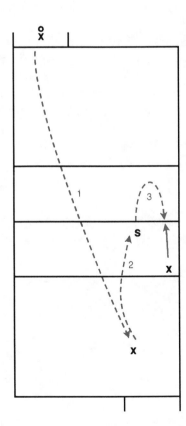

Success Goal = a. 12 out of 15 legal serves
                  b. 10 out of 12 good forearm passes
                  c. 8 out of 10 good back sets
                  d. 5 out of 8 successful attacks

Your Score = a. (#) _____ serves
               b. (#) _____ forearm passes
               c. (#) _____ back sets
               d. (#) _____ attacks

3. Continuous Three-on-Three Drill

Any number of teams of three players each line up one behind the other on the end line of one side of the court. Each team has a volleyball. Another team begins on the court on the opposite side of the net without a ball.

The first team in line serves and runs out onto their court. The ball is rallied until play is over. The team winning the rally scores a point. The winning team positions themselves on the far court. The players of the losing team return to the end of the line. The next team of three serves immediately, and the game continues.

The purpose of this game is to make it to the far side of the court and remain there as long as possible by winning rallies. On the reception of serve, the team must complete the three-hit combination—pass, set, and attack—for the rally to continue. After serve receive, the ball may be returned with less than three hits. No dinks in front of the attack line are allowed.

Success Goal = be the first team to obtain an agreed-upon number of points

Your Score = (#) _____ team points

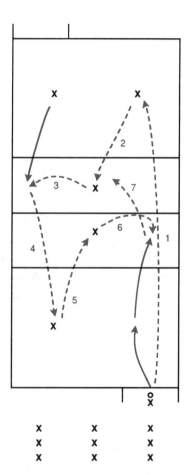

4. Attack Line Dink Game

Get together two teams of three each, one team on each side of the net. Play a game with the attack lines as the end lines.

Play is initiated with an overhead pass over the net. The receiving team must execute a three-hit combination of pass, set, and dink. The team that wins the rally wins a point. The team that loses the rally initiates the next rally with an overhead pass.

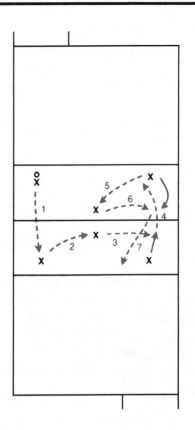

Success Goal = reach an agreed-upon number of points before your opponent

Your Score = (#) _____ team points

5. One-Third Court Game

Place yourself and three other players into two teams of two each. Play a regular volleyball game, except that the court boundaries consist of the length of the court but only one third of its width.

Play is initiated by a serve from the end line. The rally continues until an error is made and a point is won. Two points are awarded for each three-hit combination. One point is awarded for winning a rally.

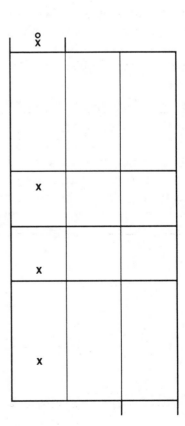

Success Goal = be the first team to earn an agreed-upon number of points

Your Score = (#) _____ team points

Step 10 Dig

The dig is the reception of the opponent's attack. It can be performed with either one or two hands. However, you should use a one-handed dig *only* in extreme emergencies. When you dig with two hands, you have much more control and ability to direct the ball as desired.

The essential element for successful digging is reading the opponent's attack to gain clues as to the direction of the upcoming spike or dink. A hard-driven spike travels so fast that it takes less than a half-second to hit the floor. This indicates that you must be in the correct defensive position to play the ball before the spike is made, because there is not enough time to move after the ball is hit.

WHY IS THE DIG IMPORTANT?

The dig is the only skill that can successfully be used to receive an attack. Players use other skills in emergency situations, but generally with limited success. Good digging is a very exciting aspect of the game and, thus, has great spectator appeal. Strong digging also tends to frustrate powerful spikers. If the attack is consistently dug, attackers begin to feel that they must change their strategy. This often results in errors by the attackers.

HOW TO EXECUTE THE DIG

The performance of the dig in volleyball is somewhat similar to that of the forearm pass. The main difference is that in the forearm pass, you have time to move, set your position, and play the ball. In the dig, however, you must react and play the ball with little time to strategically position yourself. When digging a ball, you should allow it to drop as low as possible, increasing the amount of time you have to play it. You must cushion the ball, absorbing the force from a hard-driven spike, and direct it high and toward the general vicinity of the center of the court, making it easier for your setter to play it. You should flick your wrists or flex the elbows at contact to ensure height and to ensure that the ball will remain on your side of the net (see Figure 10.1). The dig is often combined with other defensive skills, such as the sprawl and the roll (which are discussed in Step 16).

Figure 10.1   Keys to Success:
      Dig

**Preparation
Phase**

1. Hand position
2. Stride with feet shoulder
   width
3. Knees bent
4. Forearms parallel to
   thighs
5. Back straight
6. Eyes on ball

**Execution
Phase**

1. Thumbs of hands
   parallel
2. Heels of hands together
3. Reach toward ball
4. Drop shoulder closest to
   target
5. Slight extension of the
   body toward ball
6. Forward and upward
   "poking" motion
7. Flick wrists or flex
   elbows to gain greater
   height
8. Hip action is forward
9. Watch ball contact arms

**Follow-Through
Phase**

1. Forearm platform toward target
2. Arms not higher than shoulders
3. Transfer weight forward
4. Eyes follow ball to target

Detecting Dig Errors

The greatest cause for dig errors is a poor beginning defensive position. As a backcourt defensive player, you must begin near the sidelines or end lines of the court. By beginning in a position near the side- or end lines, you will be moving into the center of the court when you attempt to dig the ball. This helps you keep the ball in front of you and on the court.

ERROR 	CORRECTION
1. The ball goes straight up or back over your head.	1. Try to stop your arms on contact by using a "poking" action on the ball. Let the ball drop to waist level or lower before contact.
2. The ball is low and fast as it leaves your arms.	2. Bend your knees, keeping your back straight, as you move under the ball; touch the floor with your hands to stay in a low position.
3. You do not transfer your weight toward the intended target.	3. Check to see that your weight ends up on your forward foot and that your body is inclined forward.
4. The ball does not go high (2 or 3 feet above the net) and toward the center of the court.	4. To make the ball go high, flick your wrists or flex your elbows at contact.
5. The ball does not remain on your side of the net.	5. At contact, flick your wrists or flex your elbows.

ERROR   **CORRECTION**

6. The ball hits your arms and continues in the same direction it was already going.

6. Drop the shoulder closer to the target to change the platform angle so that it faces the target.

Dig Drills

1. *Pepper Drill*

With a partner, player A tosses the ball to him- or herself and spikes it toward player B. Player B digs the ball back to player A, who sets it to B. B then spikes the ball back to A, who digs it back to B. This nonstop action can continue indefinitely.

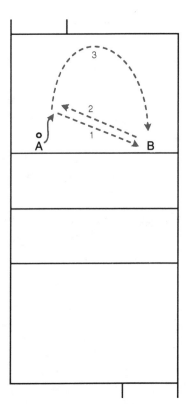

Success Goal = 5 digs within a nonstop sequence

Your Score = (#) _____ digs

2. *Digging Left Back Drill*

Begin on the left sideline approximately 20 feet from the net with your back to the sideline. A partner stands on a box, chair, or official's stand in the left forward position on the opposite side of the net.

Your partner self-tosses and spikes the ball to you. You must dig the ball 2–3 feet higher than the top of the net and toward the center of the court.

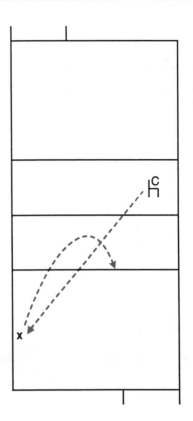

Success Goal = 6 out of 10 successful digs

Your Score = (#) _____ digs

3. *Digging Middle Back Drill*

This is the same as the previous drill, except that you stand in the center back position on the end line.

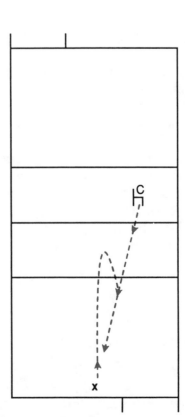

Success Goal = 6 out of 10 successful digs

Your Score = (#) _____ digs

4. *Digging Right Back Drill*

This is the same as the previous two drills, except that you stand in the right back position with your back to the sideline.

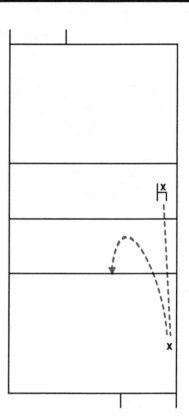

Success Goal = 6 out of 10 successful digs

Your Score = (#) _____ digs

5. *Two-Person Digging Drill*

With a partner as another defensive player, take starting positions in either of the following combinations: left back and center back, right back and center back, or left forward and left back.

Another partner, on the other side of the net as in the three previous drills, spikes the ball between your two defensive players. The defender closer to the net always crosses in front of the defender farther from the net as you both move to dig the ball.

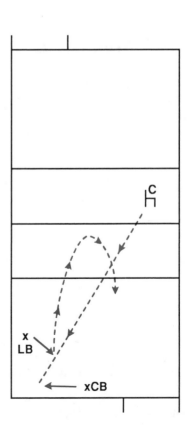

Success Goal = 5 successful digs completed
by each digger in 10 attempts

Your Score = (#) _____ digs

Dig
Keys to Success Checklist

Successful digging is dependent upon your ability to read your opponent's attack. As a digging player, you should concentrate on the opposing attacker's approach, location of the set, position of the shoulders, and arm swing. Use any clues that you can gain from these observations to determine the best starting location for all defensive players.

Use clues gained from your instructor's observations below to determine extra practice needs.

**Preparation
Phase**

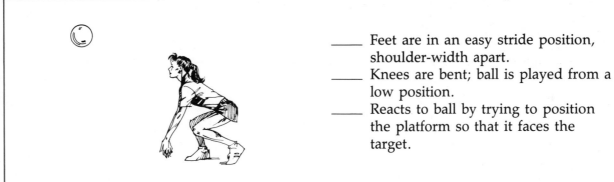

_____ Feet are in an easy stride position, shoulder-width apart.
_____ Knees are bent; ball is played from a low position.
_____ Reacts to ball by trying to position the platform so that it faces the target.

**Execution
Phase**

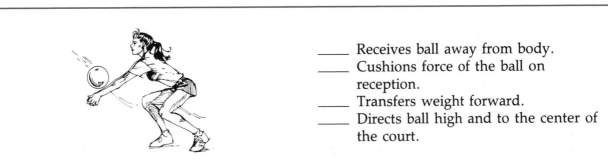

_____ Receives ball away from body.
_____ Cushions force of the ball on reception.
_____ Transfers weight forward.
_____ Directs ball high and to the center of the court.

**Follow-Through
Phase**

____ Arms remain below shoulder level.
____ Transfers weight toward target.
____ Eyes follow ball to target.

Step 11   Five-Skill Combination

You have learned to execute the three-hit combination, using the forearm pass as the first contact. Now you will practice changing from defense to offense by using the dig as the first contact. This transitional phase of the game is one of the most important. Teams that cannot convert from defense to offense successfully find it difficult to win points or gain side outs from their opponents.

WHY IS THIS FIVE-SKILL COMBINATION IMPORTANT?

If your team cannot return your opponent's attack by converting it into your own attack, you will constantly find yourselves returning free balls to your opponents. A free ball is easy to convert into an attack; therefore, your team will constantly be on the defensive.

Five-Skill Combination Drills

1. Serve, Forearm Pass, Set, Attack, and Dig Drill

In a group of five, have a server and a digger on one court and a passer, a setter, and an attacker on the opposite court.

The server underhand serves the ball to the passer, who is in the left back position of the other court. The passer forearm passes the ball to the setter, who shouldn't have to move more than a step. The setter sets high (at least 6 feet higher than the net) and outside to the attacker, positioned on the attack line at the left sideline. The attacker spikes the ball over the net to the left back area of the opponent's court. The digger plays the ball so that it is 2–3 feet higher than the top of the net and to the center of his or her own court.

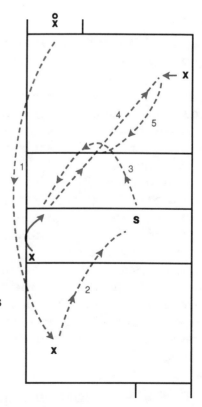

Success Goal = a. 12 out of 15 legal serves
b. 10 out of 12 good forearm passes
c. 8 out of 10 good sets
d. 6 out of 8 legal spikes
e. 4 out of 6 good digs

Your Score = a. (#) _____ serves
b. (#) _____ forearm passes
c. (#) _____ sets
d. (#) _____ spikes
e. (#) _____ digs

2. *Serve, Forearm Pass, Back Set, Attack, and Dig Drill*

This is the same as the previous drill, with the following exceptions: The passer is in right back position; the setter back sets the ball at least 5 feet above the top of the net and toward the right sideline; the attacker is positioned on the attack line at the right sideline; and the digger is in the right back position.

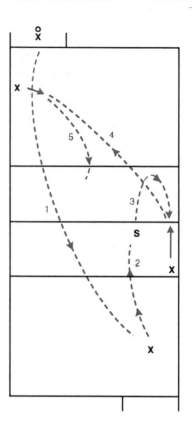

Success Goal = a. 12 out of 15 legal serves
　　　　　　　　b. 10 out of 12 good forearm passes
　　　　　　　　c. 8 out of 10 good sets
　　　　　　　　d. 6 out of 8 legal spikes
　　　　　　　　e. 4 out of 6 good digs

Your Score = a. (#) _____ serves
　　　　　　　　b. (#) _____ forearm passes
　　　　　　　　c. (#) _____ sets
　　　　　　　　d. (#) _____ spikes
　　　　　　　　e. (#) _____ digs

3. *One Setter Three-on-Three Drill*

For this drill, you need three players on each side of the court—a server, a digger, and an attacker. A seventh player acts as a setter, alternating sides of the net, depending upon the location of the ball.

The game is initiated with a serve, and the ball is rallied generally according to regular game rules. The setter, though, always assumes a position right of center front on the side of the court where the ball is being played, changing sides of the court as the ball goes over the net. The setter sets the hitters at the attack line to increase the other side's digging opportunities. The team winning a rally scores a point. The team losing the rally makes the next serve.

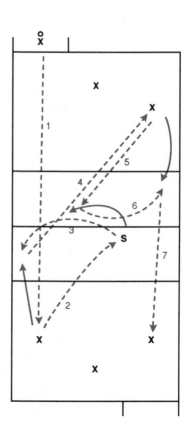

Success Goal = be the first team to reach a predetermined number of points

Your Score = (#) _____ team points

4. Diggers and Receivers Drill

For this drill you need two teams of five players each on opposite sides of the net. Team A has a server, three diggers, and a setter. Team B has two serve receivers, two attackers, and a setter.

Team A serves; team B receives, setting up an attack with the set being made to the attack line. Team A digs the ball and sets at least 7 feet higher than the top of the net so that the ball lands on or within 1 foot of the left sideline (no further attack).

Team A serves 5 times, and then the two teams reverse roles. The receiving team gets 1 point for a successful attack, and the digging team gets 1 point for a successful dig and set.

Success Goal = be the first team to reach a predetermined number of points

Your Score = (#) _____ team points

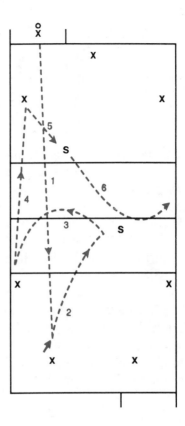

Step 12 On-Hand and Off-Hand Spiking

When attacking, you hit the ball *on-hand* when the setter is on the same side as your hitting hand. This means that the set does not have to cross in front of your body before you make contact. If you are right-handed, you hit on-hand when in the left forward position; if left-handed, you hit on-hand when in the right forward position.

You attack the ball off-hand when the setter is on the opposite side from your hitting hand. If right-handed, you hit an off-hand spike when in the right forward position; if left-handed, you hit an off-hand spike when in the left forward position.

WHY ARE ON-HAND AND OFF-HAND SPIKES IMPORTANT?

The on-hand spike is important because it is the easiest spike for you to perform. Also, it is the most powerful attack. You should be capable of directing the spike to any area of the opponent's court.

The off-hand spike is important due to the rotation of positions in volleyball; you are re-quired to spike efficiently from both sides of the court. Another important consideration is in the determination of the lineup. A coach would like to have the left-handers specialize as right-side attackers and the right-handers specialize as left-side attackers.

HOW TO EXECUTE ON-HAND AND OFF-HAND SPIKES

You execute both the on-hand and off-hand spikes in the same manner as the hard-driven spike. The only difference is the location of the ball in relation to your arm and body (see the Execution Phase of Figure 12.1). When you perform on-hand, contact the cross-court spike directly in front of your hitting shoulder and direct it toward the long diagonal part of the court. The down-the-line spike is contacted at the midline of your body.

When you perform off-hand, contact the cross-court spike more toward the midline of your body. In the down-the-line spike, contact the ball in front of your hitting shoulder.

Figure 12.1 Keys to Success: Spike

Preparation Phase

1. Weight forward
2. Watch the setter
3. Eyes on the ball after set
4. Wait on attack line
5. Anticipate approach

**Execution
Phase**

1. Begin approach when ball is at peak of its trajectory
2. Cover distance with few steps
3. Last two steps right and close left or step to jump
4. Arms swing back to waist level

5. Both arms swing forward
6. Both arms swing high toward ball
7. Contact ball in front of hitting shoulder
8. Contact with heel of open hand
9. Contact at center back

a

On-Hand, Down-the-Line

*Right-Handed
Player*

*Left-Handed
Player*

10. Contact down-the-line spikes toward midline of body

b

On-Hand, Cross-Court

*Right-Handed
Player*

*Left-Handed
Player*

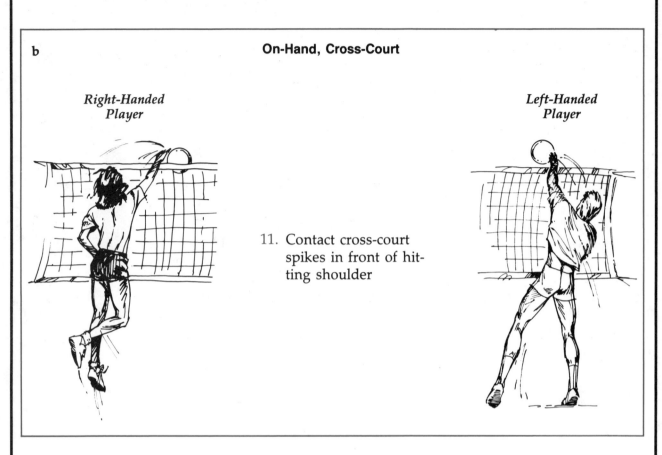

11. Contact cross-court spikes in front of hitting shoulder

c

Off-Hand, Down-the-Line

*Right-Handed
Player*

*Left-Handed
Player*

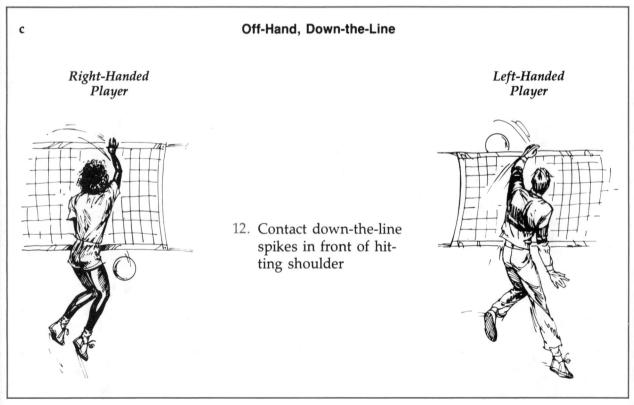

12. Contact down-the-line spikes in front of hitting shoulder

d

Off-Hand, Cross-Court

Right-Handed Player

Left-Handed Player

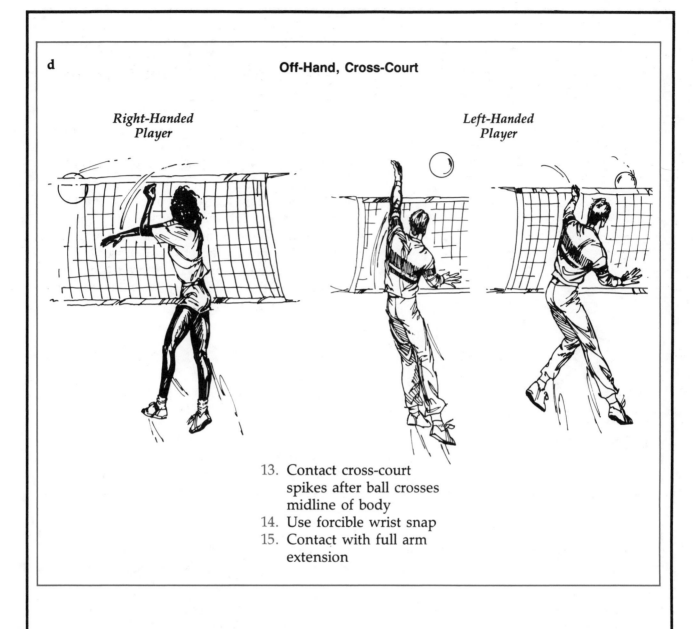

13. Contact cross-court spikes after ball crosses midline of body
14. Use forcible wrist snap
15. Contact with full arm extension

Follow-Through Phase

1. Hand follows ball to target
2. Land on both feet

3. Bend knees to cushion landing

Detecting On-Hand and Off-Hand Spike Errors

It is extremely important that you recognize the difference between hitting on-hand and hitting off-hand. You must understand where the ball should be in order to successfully direct it either cross-court or down the line. Example: If a right-handed left forward player hitting on-hand desires to make a down-the-line spike and contacts the ball in front of the hitting shoulder instead of more toward the midline of the body, the spike will go toward the center back of the court.

ERROR

CORRECTION

ERROR	CORRECTION
1. The ball goes into the net.	1. You should contact the ball just in front of your hitting shoulder; the farther the ball is in front of you, the lower it drops before contact and the greater the chance of its being hit into the net.
2. You stop approach and wait for the ball.	2. You should not begin your approach until the ball is half the distance to you from the setter.
3. You contact the net.	3. The set must be at least 1 foot from the net. You must execute a heel plant to change horizontal momentum into vertical momentum.
4. The ball goes out-of-bounds over the end line.	4. You *must* contact the ball in front of your hitting shoulder. Your wrist snaps your hand over the top of the ball.
5. You lack height on your jump.	5. You must plant your heels to convert horizontal momentum into vertical momentum. Both arms must swing forcibly upward.
6. The set goes by you.	6. You must wait at the attack line until you know where the set will be located.

ERROR

7. The ball does not stay within 2 feet and parallel to the sideline in the down-the-line spike.

8. The ball does not go diagonally to the opposite corner of the court.

CORRECTION

7. When you hit on-hand, the ball must pass your hitting shoulder and be contacted more toward the midline of your body. When you hit off-hand, the ball crosses the midline of your body and is contacted in front of your hitting shoulder.

8. When hitting on-hand, you should hit the ball in front of your hitting shoulder. When hitting off-hand, you should hit the ball after it crosses the midline of your body.

Spike Drills

1. Spiking From a Set Drill

Get together a group of four: a tosser on one side of the net and a receiver, a setter, and an attacker on the opposite side. Set up a 2-foot wide target parallel to the right sideline.

The tosser throws the ball hard over the net to the receiver, who is standing in the back court. The receiver forearm passes the ball to the setter at the net right of center front, who sets the ball high outside to the attacker waiting at the attack line. The attacker should try spiking the ball over the net both down-the-line into the target and cross-court into the back one-third corner of the opponent's side.

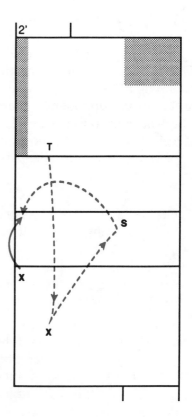

Success Goal = a. 4 out of 5 accurate down-the-line spikes
b. 4 out of 5 accurate cross-court spikes

Your Score = a. (#) _____ down-the-line spikes
b. (#) _____ cross-court spikes

2. *Spiking From a Back Set Drill*

This is the same as the previous drill, with the following exceptions: The setter is right of center front and must back set the ball at least 5 feet higher than the net to the attacker, who must be at the attack line on the right sideline.

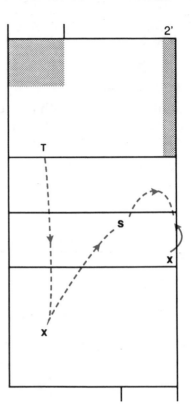

Success Goal = a. 4 out of 5 accurate down-the-line spikes
b. 4 out of 5 accurate cross-court spikes

Your Score = a. (#) _____ down-the-line spikes
b. (#) _____ cross-court spikes

3. *Spike Hit for Direction Drill*

With a partner near the net as a setter, you be a spiker at the attack line near either sideline. Place two 10-foot-square targets in the back corners of the opponent's court.

Pass the ball high to the setter. The setter sets the ball back to you. Without jumping, spike the ball over the net to either of two large target areas.

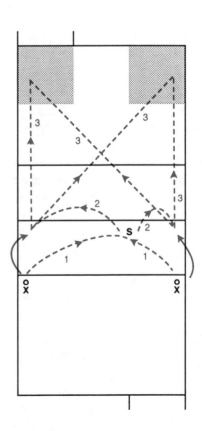

Success Goal = a. 5 out of 10 spike hits landing on the left back target area
b. 5 out of 10 spike hits landing on the right back target area

Your Score = a. (#) _____ spike hits landing on the left target
b. (#) _____ spike hits landing on the right target

4. *Pressure Spiking Drill*

Have three spikers line up one behind the other at the attack line on the left sideline. A tosser stands at the net, and additional players are needed as ball retrievers and feeders for the tosser.

The tosser continuously tosses balls high to the sideline. The first player approaches, spikes, and returns to the end of the line by making a circle in the clockwise direction. Second player immediately follows and spikes, followed by the third player. Action is continuous with the time between tosses as minimal as possible until 30 tosses have been made. Retrievers and feeders must get balls back to the tosser as quickly as possible.

This drill can be executed by using either a down-the-line spike or a cross-court spike to a 10-foot-square target in the opposite corner of the court. The spikers should practice approaching from both sidelines.

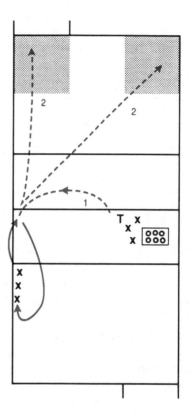

Success Goal = 10 good spikes by the group into the designated target out of 30 attempts

Your Score = (#) _____ good spikes by the group

On-Hand and Off-Hand Spikes Keys to Success Checklist

Success in directing on-hand or off-hand spikes either down-the-line or cross-court is determined by your ability to decide where to contact the ball in relation to your hitting hand and the midline of your body. Asterisks indicate that several items on this checklist are the same as they were for the hard-driven spike in Step 8. The observer should pay particular attention to the items on the checklist that deal with location of contact in relation to the desired direction of the spike.

Preparation Phase

* ____ Weight is forward, attacker ready to move.
* ____ Attacker remains at sideline until beginning approach.

* ____ Attacker watches setter until the ball is set, then focuses on the ball.
* ____ Attacker waits at attack line until set is half the distance from the setter to the attacker.

Execution Phase

* ____ Approach begins when set is half the distance from the setter to attacker.
* ____ Last two steps of approach are step right and close left or step to jump.
* ____ Both arms swing back to waist height, then forward and up.
* ____ Heels are planted to convert horizontal momentum into vertical momentum.

* ____ Weight transfers to balls of feet and arms swing forward and up.
* ____ Ball is contacted with the heel of open hand, quickly followed by a snap of the wrist directing the hand over the top of the ball.

On-Hand, Down-the-Line

Right-Handed Player

Left-Handed Player

____ When the attacker hits on-hand down-the-line, the ball passes the hitting shoulder and is contacted more toward the midline of the body.

On-Hand, Cross-Court

Right-Handed Player

Left-Handed Player

_____ When the attacker hits on-hand cross-court, the ball should be contacted in front of the hitting shoulder.

Off-Hand, Down-the-Line

Right-Handed Player

Left-Handed Player

_____ When the attacker hits off-hand down-the-line, the ball crosses the midline of the body and is contacted in front of the hitting shoulder.

Off-Hand, Cross-Court

Right-Handed Player

Left-Handed Player

_____ When the attacker hits off-hand cross-court, the ball should be contacted after it crosses the midline of the body.

Follow-Through Phase

* _____ Hand follows through in the direction of the spike and drops to the waist.

* _____ Lands on two feet.
* _____ Knees bend on contact with floor to absorb force.

Step 13 Block

The block is the first line of defense against your opponent's attack. The purpose of the block is to take a portion of your court away from the opponents. A block can be considered successful if the ball rebounds off the blocker's hands directly back into the opponent's court or if the blocker deflects the ball so that it goes high in the air on the blocker's team's side of the court.

In a *single block,* only one player blocks at a time. Single blocking in volleyball is often not enough to stop the opposing attack. The purpose of the block is to take away as much court as possible from the attacker. Therefore, the wider the block, the less court the remaining defensive players must cover. Teams often join two or three players together, forming double or triple blocks, referred to as *multiple blocks.*

WHY ARE SINGLE AND MULTIPLE BLOCKS IMPORTANT?

If your block prevents the ball from entering your side of the court, this forces your opponents to set their attack a second time. This is very important because the longer your opponents play the ball, the greater the chance they will make an error, thus giving your team a point or a side out. Even if you deflect the ball into your own side of the court, if you deflect the ball high, the block is considered successful because it allows the other defensive players behind you more time to play the less forceful ball.

The greater the territory that can be eliminated from the attacker, the easier it is to defend the remaining court. If time allows players to get into position, you should always employ at least a double block. The time it is most difficult to use a multiple block is when defending the quick attack, which usually occurs near the middle of the court. Teams often use a single block in the middle of the court, using a multiple block near the sidelines.

HOW TO EXECUTE A SINGLE BLOCK

As the blocker, begin by standing within 1 foot of the net, facing the opposite court. Your hands are out to your sides at shoulder level, palms facing forward with fingers spread wide. Watching the opposing setter, wait until the ball is set to the hitter across the net from your position on the court, then change to watch the attacker until the ball comes into view. Attempt to line up one-half body width toward the opponent's hitting side.

Immediately after the attacker jumps, bend your knees and jump. Reach over the top of the net, your hands penetrating into your opponent's court, and position your hands to both sides of the attacker's hitting arm. Attempt to make the ball rebound off your hands back into the opponent's court. Return to the floor with a two-footed landing. Immediately turn off the net to locate the position of the ball (see Figure 13.1).

Figure 13.1 Keys to Success:
Single Block

Preparation Phase

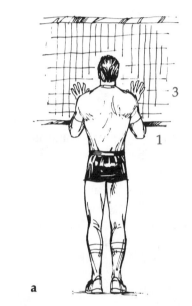

1. Wait at the net
2. Watch the opposing setter
3. Hands at shoulder level
4. After set, eyes focus on opposing attacker
5. Position on attacker's hitting arm

Execution Phase

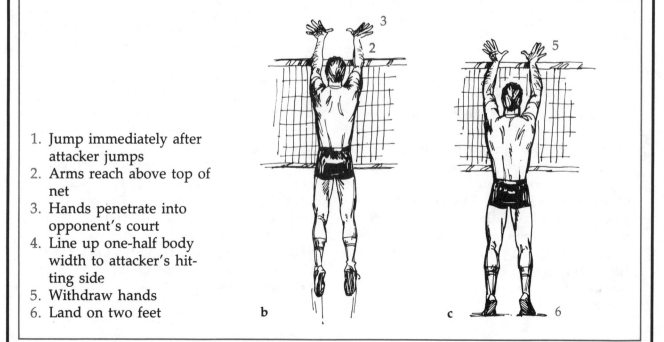

1. Jump immediately after attacker jumps
2. Arms reach above top of net
3. Hands penetrate into opponent's court
4. Line up one-half body width to attacker's hitting side
5. Withdraw hands
6. Land on two feet

Follow-Through Phase

1. Bend knees to cushion landing
2. Turn away from net
3. Look for ball

d

HOW TO EXECUTE MULTIPLE BLOCKS

The execution of the double and triple blocks are similar to the execution of the single block. The main difference is that two or three players join together to block (see Figure 13.2). When the block is on the outside of the court, the outside player sets the block and the middle player joins the outside player. When moving to join the outside player, the middle player should watch the outside player moving to that position; then both players can jump at the same time. The outside player's hands are directly lined up with the ball, and the middle player's hands take away the cross-court angle.

When the middle blocker is blocking and the opponent's set is high enough, both outside players move to join the middle player, forming a triple block. During this block, the middle blocker's hands directly line up with the ball, and the outside blockers take away the angles.

Figure 13.2 *Keys to Success:* *Multiple Block*

Preparation Phase

1. After the set the moving blocker focuses on the player setting the block

a

Execution Phase

1. Both blockers jump simultaneously

b

**Follow-Through
Phase**

1. All players return to
their original positions

Detecting Blocking Errors

Mistakes in blocking can be grouped in two categories—errors in technique and errors in timing. Errors in timing usually result in players missing the block completely. Errors in technique often result in the ball being deflected in such a manner that it is difficult for the backcourt defensive players to react. Whenever blockers eliminate an area of the court from the attack, the block can be considered successful, even though the blockers may not contact the ball because back row defensive players have less court area to cover.

ERROR   **CORRECTION**

1. You, the blocker, jump before the attack is completed.

2. You return to the floor while the attacker is contacting the ball.

1. Watch the opposing setter until you know where the set will be placed; then watch the attacker until the attacker's hand and the ball are both in view.

2. Wait to jump until just after the attacker jumps.

ERROR   **CORRECTION**

3. The fingers of your hands are closed.

3. Spread the fingers of your hands wide so that your thumbs are pointing at the ceiling.

4. You land with straight legs.

4. You must bend your knees upon landing for cushioning.

5. You line up body-to-body with the attacker.

5. Line up one-half body width on the attacker's hitting side.

6. As the joining blocker, you move into the teammate setting the block.

6. You should focus on the player setting the block, not on the ball.

ERROR 🚫

CORRECTION

7. The ball contacts your hands and remains on your side of the net.

7. You must square your shoulders to the net before jumping.

8. As the joining blocker, you reach toward the attacker's hitting hand (see Error 7).

8. As the joining blocker, you are protecting the angle only and should not reach for the ball.

Blocking Drills

1. Toss to Block Drill

Have a partner be a tosser on one side of the net; you be a blocker on the opposite side.

The tosser, using a two-handed overhead throw, jumps and throws the ball over the net in a downward motion. Jump and attempt to block the ball before it penetrates the net. The blocked ball should land within the boundaries of the opposite court.

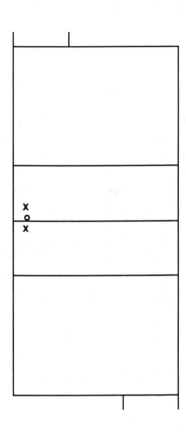

Success Goal = 6 out of 10 good blocks

Your Score = (#) _____ blocks

2. Blind Blocking Drill

For this drill you need a group of three—the blocker (yourself) and a tosser on one side of the net, and a spiker on the opposite side of the net.

From a position behind you, the tosser throws the ball over the net, high and relatively close to the net. The attacker jumps and spikes the ball, aiming at you, the blocker. Jump and attempt to block the ball back at the attacker; it should land inbounds.

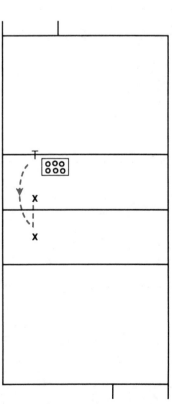

Success Goal = 4 out of 10 good blocks

Your Score = (#) _____ blocks

3. Double Blocking Drill

Have a group of four take the roles of a tosser and an attacker on one side of the net, and two blockers (including you) on the opposite side. One blocker should be near the middle of the court, the other near the sideline.

The tosser tosses the ball high and outside to the attacker, who is near their sideline at the attack line. The attacker approaches and spikes the ball over the net. The middle blocker joins the outside blocker, who has set the block, to form a double block.

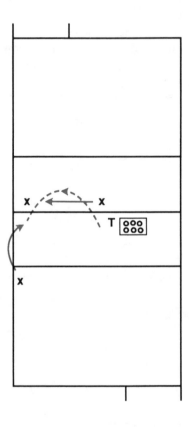

Success Goal = 4 out of 10 successful blocks

Your Score = (#) _____ blocks

4. *Endurance Blocking Drill*

This drill requires a group of eight players—two combination blockers/hitters, one setter, and one overhead passer on each side of the net. Passers should have a supply of balls (at least 10) readily available. On one side of the net, team A's two hitters begin on the attack line (see diagram), the setter at the net. On the opposite side of the net, team B's two blockers are in a ready position, the setter in the right back position. Both passers are in their respective backcourt areas.

The passer on the hitters' side (team A) begins the drill by passing the ball high to the setter, who sets either hitter. The blockers on team B react with a single block if it is a quick set, or a double block if it is a high, outside set or back set. The blocked ball should land in the attackers' court; the attackers don't need to return it.

The team B passer immediately overhead passes another ball high to the penetrating setter, who sets one of the team B hitters (in the role of blocker just seconds before). The team A blockers (earlier, hitters) react to the attack with a good block. The drill continues indefinitely, the hitters and blockers constantly changing roles like this.

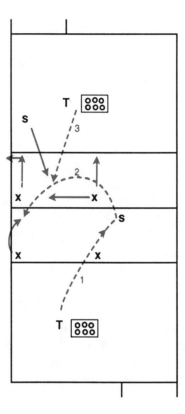

Success Goal = 5 successful blocks by your team

Your Score = (#) _____ attempts necessary to make 5 good blocks

Blocking
Keys to Success Checklist

As with the dig, a good deal of successful blocking is based on your ability to read your opponent's attack. The biggest error committed by a beginner is tending to follow the trajectory of the ball rather than concentrating on the attacker for whom he or she is responsible. One of the strongest indications that you may be doing this is if you often attempt to block even when the attacker does not complete the attack. Unnecessarily blocking and touching the net is considered to be an extremely costly error.

Have a skilled volleyball person evaluate your blocking form with this checklist.

Preparation Phase

_____ Blocker focuses on setter until the set is made, then focuses on the attacker.
_____ Blocker positions one-half body width to the attacker's hitting side.

_____ When multiple blocking, moving blocker focuses on player setting the block.
_____ In waiting position, hands are at the sides, shoulder level, and fingers spread.

Execution Phase

_____ Blocker jumps just after attacker jumps.
_____ Hands penetrate into opponent's court.

_____ In multiple blocking, all blockers jump simultaneously.
_____ Hands withdrawn as blocker returns to floor.
_____ Blocker lands on two feet.

Follow-Through Phase

____ Blocker turns off net quickly and looks for ball.

____ Knees bent to cushion landing.
____ Returns to original position.

Single Block

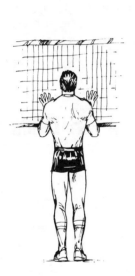   

Multiple Block

Step 14 Six-Skill Combination

Now that you have mastered the basic skills of volleyball, you can begin to move into gamelike situations. During actual competition, one play sequence can include a serve, which is forearm passed to the setter, who sets to the attacker, who attempts to hit into the opponent's court, where the opponents defend with a block and/or a dig. This sequence happens continually throughout a game.

WHY IS THIS SIX-SKILL COMBINATION IMPORTANT?

This sequence is the basis of the game of volleyball. Each time a team receives the ball from the opponents, they attempt to make the transition to offense with a forearm pass, a set, and an attack. At the same time, the opposing team is setting their defense, consisting of blocking and backcourt play. In order for the game to flow, teams must master this sequence of play.

Six-Skill Combination Drills

1. Combining Six Skills Drill

In a group of six, have a server, a blocker, and a digger on one side of the net; and a passer, a setter, and an attacker on the other side.

The server serves an underhand serve to the right back of the court. The passer forearm passes the ball to the setter, who sets high and outside to the attacker. The attacker spikes the ball over the net on the diagonal toward the digger. The blocker and the digger each attempt to play the ball. The blocker tries to keep the ball on the opponent's side. If this fails, the digger should place the ball high to the center of the digger's side of the court.

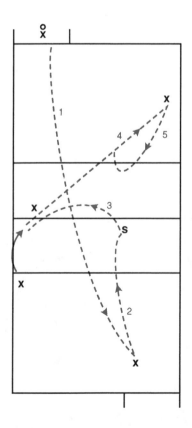

Success Goal = a. 10 out of 12 good serves
b. 8 out of 10 successful forearm pass-set-spike combinations
c. 5 out of 10 successful blocks or digs

Your Score = a. (#) _____ serves
b. (#) _____ forearm pass-set-spike combinations
c. (#) _____ blocks
d. (#) _____ digs

2. Combining Six Skills, Back Set Drill

This is the same as the previous drill, with the exception that the serve goes to the left back of the court, the setter back sets, and the attacker hits from the right sideline on the diagonal.

Success Goal = a. 10 out of 12 good serves
b. 8 out of 10 successful forearm pass-set-spike combinations
c. 5 out of 10 successful blocks or digs

Your Score = a. (#) ____ serves
b. (#) ____ forearm pass-set-spike combinations
c. (#) ____ blocks
d. (#) ____ digs

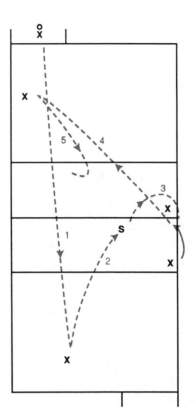

3. Five-Player Reception Drill

Six players set up on each side of the court. The server on one side serves underhand. The receiving team—in the W-formation—attempts a pass-set-spike combination, the set going alternately to the left forward and right forward and the spike going on the diagonal. The serving team attempts to block with a double block. Any ball not successfully blocked should be dug high to the center of the digger's side.

Success Goal = a. 10 out of 12 good serves
b. 8 out of 10 accurate forearm pass-set-spike combinations
c. 5 out of 10 successful blocks or digs

Your Score = a. (#) ____ serves
b. (#) ____ forearm pass-set-spike combinations
c. (#) ____ blocks
d. (#) ____ digs

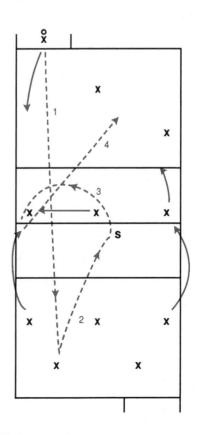

4. Six-Player Modified Game

Six players set up on each side of the court. The player in each center front position is the team's setter. The W-formation is used for serve reception. Each team makes 5 consecutive serves. After 10 serves, the players on both teams rotate one position clockwise.

The ball is rallied as in a regular volleyball game. The team that wins the rally scores a point. When a team successfully completes a pass-set-spike combination, they score an additional point. For a bad serve, subtract a point from the team's score.

Success Goal = be the team earning the greater number of points after six rotations (60 total serves)

Your Score = (#) _____ team points

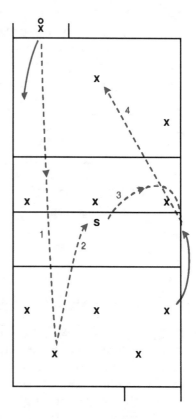

Step 15   Advanced Serves

You hit the *topspin serve* hard and impart forward spin on the ball, causing it to drop quickly into the opponent's court after it crosses the net. This serve travels a true course once it is directed because spin stabilizes the ball, unlike with the floater serve.

The last serve for you to master is the *roundhouse floater serve.* Players often find it easy to get this serve over the net because it utilizes the larger muscle groups of the body. Even though it is easy to impart the force necessary to get the ball over the net, the form is not typical of such other overhand sport movements as throwing, which adds to the complexity of the learning process. The ball floats and knuckles the same as the overhand floater serve. The roundhouse floater is used extensively by the Japanese.

WHY ARE THE TOPSPIN AND ROUNDHOUSE FLOATER SERVES IMPORTANT?

The topspin serve causes the ball to travel very rapidly and drop quickly, which means that the opposing team has little time to react. This catches the opponents off guard, and the serve may be an ace (a serve that either is not touched at all by the receiving team or is touched by one player in a manner that prevents any further play on the ball). It is also difficult for defenders to judge whether a topspin serve will land in or out when it approaches the end line. Serves that appear to be out often drop quickly at the last second and land within the court boundaries.

The roundhouse floater serve can often be executed even if you have difficulty performing the overhand serve; because you use larger muscle groups in this serve, you do not need as much strength. You may thus find initial success with this serve before you are able to execute the overhand serve.

One negative aspect of the roundhouse floater, though, is that you do not have your eyes on the target area of the opponent's court. Furthermore, remember that it is wise to be able to execute more than one type of serve because a variety is more effective in keeping the opposition off-balance.

HOW TO EXECUTE THE TOPSPIN SERVE

The topspin serve is similar in execution to the other serves. In the beginning position, turn your shoulders slightly to the sideline. Point your forward foot toward a net post. Place the ball toss slightly behind your hitting shoulder. Contact the ball just below its center back with your arm at full extension; immediately follow with a wrist snap, causing the fingers to roll over the top of the ball. The hitting hand forcibly drops down to the waist (see Figure 15.1).

Figure 15.1 Keys to Success: *Topspin Serve*

Preparation Phase

1. Stride position
2. Shoulders angle to sideline
3. Feet angle to sideline
4. Eyes on ball toss position

Execution Phase

1. Toss ball behind hitting shoulder
2. Arm swings back
3. Elbow high
4. Hand to ear
5. Contact at full extension
6. Contact with heel of open hand
7. Arch back
8. Snap wrist
9. Fingers over top of ball

**Follow-Through
Phase**

1. Transfer weight to forward foot
2. Arm forcibly to waist
3. Move onto court

Detecting Topspin Serve Errors

The topspin serve is a difficult serve to master because proper hand contact with the ball, the amount of wrist snap, and where the ball is contacted in relation to your hitting shoulder are all critical. A slight deviation from the proper technique can cause an extreme deviation in the resulting serve. For example, if your hand contacts the center back of the ball instead of below center back, the topspin will cause the ball to drop too quickly, and it will not clear the net.

ERROR

CORRECTION

1. The ball goes into the net.

2. The ball goes to the right.

3. The serve does not reach the net.

1. You must toss the ball behind the shoulder of your hitting hand.

2. The toss must be in front of your body, not outside your hitting shoulder.

3. Transfer your weight at contact. Contact the ball with the heel of an open hand.

ERROR	CORRECTION
4. The ball goes over the end line of the opponent's court.	4. Contact the ball below center back, and snap your wrist forcibly, rolling your fingers over the top of the ball, finishing by dropping the hitting hand to your waist.
5. You take two or three steps to serve the ball.	5. Toss the ball slightly behind your shoulder and transfer your weight forward.

Topspin Serve
Keys to Success Checklist

As indicated in the discussion of the overhand floater serve, the ability to toss the ball consistently is essential to successful serving. In fact, the toss is even more critical in performing the topspin serve. You must contact the ball slightly behind your hitting shoulder and slightly below the center back of the ball; otherwise, the topspin will cause the ball to drop before it reaches the net.

Have someone use this checklist to assess your technique.

**Preparation
Phase**

_____ Feet are in a comfortable stride position.
_____ Weight is evenly distributed.
_____ Shoulders and feet angle toward sideline.
_____ Eyes are on the ball toss position.

**Execution
Phase**

_____ Ball is tossed slightly behind hitting shoulder, with little or no spin.
_____ Hitting arm swings back with elbow high and hand close to ear.
_____ Ball is contacted with heel of open hand, with arm fully extended.
_____ Wrist snaps forcibly.
_____ Eyes are on ball until contact.

**Follow-Through
Phase**

_____ Arm drops to waist.
_____ Server moves onto court.

HOW TO EXECUTE THE ROUND-HOUSE FLOATER SERVE

Stand facing the sideline with your forward foot toward a net post. Toss the ball slightly ahead of your body, away from the midline and toward your nonhitting shoulder. Fully extend your arm throughout the entire motion of the serve. Your arm drops back and then swings up over your head, making contact with the ball directly in front of your body. As your arm swings, your weight shifts forward onto your front foot, and your hips rotate forward, immediately followed by your shoulder bringing your hitting arm into contact with the ball. The contact is with an open hand just below the center back of the ball, a ''poking'' action with no wrist snap and little follow-through. Turn your body and move toward the court (see Figure 15.2).

Figure 15.2 Keys to Success:
Roundhouse
Floater Serve

**Preparation
Phase**

1. Stagger stride
2. Shoulders angle to sideline
3. Feet angle to sideline
4. Eyes on ball

**Execution
Phase**

1. Toss ball in front of body
2. Toss ball closer to non-hitting shoulder
3. Arm drops back
4. Arm fully extended until contact
5. Contact with heel of open hand
6. No wrist snap
7. Body rotates into contact

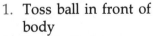

**Follow-Through
Phase**

1. Transfer weight to forward foot
2. Slight follow-through of the arm
3. Turn and move onto court

Detecting Roundhouse Floater Serve Errors

Errors in roundhouse serving are usually associated with the inability to toss the ball consistently. If you toss the ball behind or too close to your body, the resultant serve will be out-of-bounds over your opponent's end line. As in the execution of all serves, you should try to develop a consistent form for execution. The elimination of extraneous movements helps to increase serving success.

ERROR

1. The ball goes into the net.

2. The serve does not reach the net.

CORRECTION

1. The toss is too far ahead of your non-hitting shoulder or the toss may be too low.

2. Rotate your body into contact and contact the ball with the heel of an open hand.

ERROR   **CORRECTION**

3. The ball goes over the end line of the opponent's court.

4. You take two or three steps to serve the ball.

3. Contact the ball to the nonhitting side of your body, just below the center back of the ball.

4. The toss must be between the midline of your body and your nonhitting shoulder, as well as close to your body. Steps are extraneous.

Roundhouse Floater Serve Keys to Success Checklist

The roundhouse floater serve is most effective if you are capable of creating true floating action on the ball. This action is highly dependent upon hand–ball contact. When the ball leaves your hand, it must not be spinning. A spinning ball is stable and does not float. It is the floating, knuckling action that makes this serve most effective.

Have a skilled observer assess your performance with the criteria below.

Preparation Phase

_____ Feet are in a comfortable stride position.
_____ Weight is evenly distributed.
_____ Shoulders and feet angle toward sideline.
_____ Eyes are on the ball.

Execution
Phase

_____ Ball is tossed between the midline of the body and the nonhitting shoulder, with little or no spin.
_____ Hitting arm is fully extended throughout the action.
_____ Ball is contacted with heel of an open hand.
_____ Eyes are on the ball until contact.

Follow-Through
Phase

_____ There is little follow-through of the arm.
_____ Server rotates body and moves onto the court.

Advanced Serve Drills

1. Wall Serve Drill

Stand in a serving position approximately 20 feet from a wall on which is a marked line of the proper net height. Toss and serve the ball into the wall. Try both topspin and round-house floater serves.

Success Goal = a. 9 out of 10 good topspin serves

b. 9 out of 10 good roundhouse floater serves

Your Score = a. (#) _____ topspin serves

b. (#) _____ roundhouse floater serves

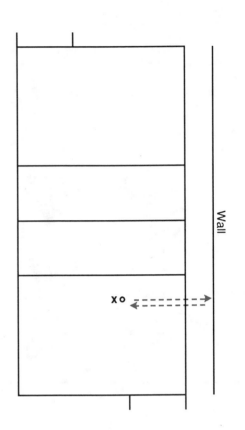

2. Partner Serve at the Net Drill

At a distance of 20 feet from the net, serve the ball over the net without its touching the net, to a partner standing 20 feet on the other side. Your partner must be able to catch the ball without moving more than one step in any direction.

Success Goal = a. 7 out of 10 accurate topspin serve attempts

b. 7 out of 10 good roundhouse floater serves

Your Score = a. (#) _____ topspin serves

b. (#) _____ roundhouse floater serves

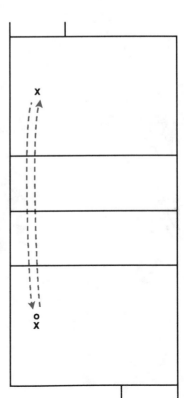

3. End Line Serve Drill

You and a partner stand on opposite end lines and serve back and forth. Try both types of advanced serves. Your serves may land any-where within the boundaries of the other's side.

Success Goal = a. 9 out of 10 good topspin serves
b. 9 out of 10 good roundhouse floater serves

Your Score = a. (#) _____ topspin serves
b. (#) _____ roundhouse floater serves

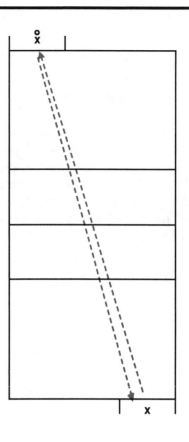

4. Consistency Drill

This is the same as the previous drill, but with different Success Goals.

Success Goal = a. 25 consecutive good topspin serves
b. 25 consecutive good roundhouse floater serves

Your Score = a. (#) _____ consecutive topspin serves
b. (#) _____ consecutive roundhouse floater serves

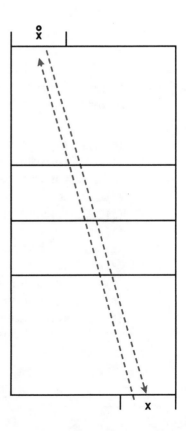

5. Serve for Accuracy Drill

Place a target sheet approximately 10-feet square in one of the six rotational positions. On the opposite side of the court, stand in the serving area (right one-third of the court) and serve, attempting to hit the target. This drill should be attempted with the target in each of the six areas.

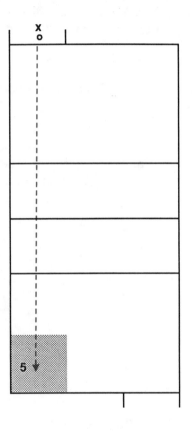

Success Goal = a. hit the target with 5 topspin serves out of 20 attempts
             b. hit the target with 5 roundhouse floater serves out of 20 attempts

Your Score = a. (#) _____ topspin serves hitting target 1
              (#) _____ topspin serves hitting target 2
              (#) _____ topspin serves hitting target 3
              (#) _____ topspin serves hitting target 4
              (#) _____ topspin serves hitting target 5
              (#) _____ topspin serves hitting target 6
        b. (#) _____ roundhouse floater serves hitting target 1
              (#) _____ roundhouse floater serves hitting target 2
              (#) _____ roundhouse floater serves hitting target 3
              (#) _____ roundhouse floater serves hitting target 4
              (#) _____ roundhouse floater serves hitting target 5
              (#) _____ roundhouse floater serves hitting target 6

6. Team Serving Drill

In two teams of six each, one team groups in each service area of the court. Have plenty of volleyballs at each serving area, an equal number at each. Place 10-foot–square targets in the same rotational positions on each side of the court.

Two or three servers on each team begin serving at the target all at the same time. After serving, each player retrieves a ball and prepares to serve again. Meanwhile, other team members will step forward to serve. Servers continuously switch places after each repetition. Repeat this drill for all six target areas.

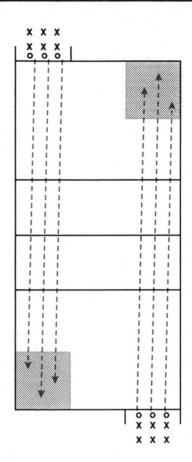

Success Goal = hit the target with 20 serves prior to your opponents for each of the six areas

Your Score = (#) _____ serves hitting target 1
(#) _____ serves hitting target 2
(#) _____ serves hitting target 3
(#) _____ serves hitting target 4
(#) _____ serves hitting target 5
(#) _____ serves hitting target 6

7. Minus Two Drill

This is almost the same as the previous drill. Here the serve needs to be only within the boundaries of the opposite court. Only one person serves at a time on each side. Each person serves only once before the next person immediately serves once. Retrieve a ball after you've served.

For each legal serve, your team scores 1 point. For every bad serve, your team is penalized 2 points. The first team to reach 20 points wins.

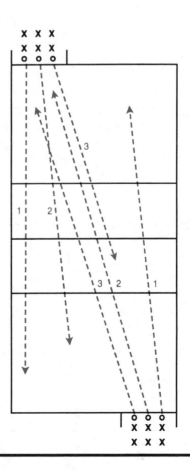

Success Goal = 20 team points

Your Score = (#) _____ team points

Step 16 Additional Individual Defense Skills

Two additional methods of individual defense are the roll and the sprawl. The *roll* is the preferred method because it allows you to return to your feet more quickly than the sprawl. The roll is used to recover when your body contacts the floor after digging the ball. It is similar to a forward roll and is done in such a way that padded body parts (those protected with extra layers of muscle) cushion your contact with the floor. The roll is not a method of digging, but rather a method of recovery.

The *sprawl* is a recent defensive technique probably coming into existence due to players' lack of strength in executing the dive. Female players especially are often more comfortable executing the sprawl. It is used mostly when necessary to play a ball in front of you, but you can also use it to play balls to either side. Like other defensive techniques, you use the sprawl when you need to move quite a distance before getting close enough to play the ball. It is used more frequently to receive a spiked ball.

WHY ARE THE ROLL AND THE SPRAWL IMPORTANT?

The rolling technique is important because it aids you in returning to your feet as quickly as possible. It is also a method of falling that allows you to cushion the landing; thus, it helps to prevent injury. You would be likely to use the roll after you have had to chase the ball from your starting defensive position some distance to either side.

The sprawl is important because it allows you to dig balls that under normal conditions would not be receivable. It also is an option for playing the ball without resorting to the dive, which proves to be very difficult for players who have weak arms. The sprawl allows you to dig the ball from a low posture, contacting the floor with a sliding motion, thereby defusing the force of impact and preventing injury.

HOW TO EXECUTE THE ROLL

There have been several different methods of performing the roll in volleyball. Current thought is that the method of roll is not of great importance, but rather the body position from which you execute the roll. The primary aspect to successful rolling is to get as close as possible to the ball, letting it drop low, and digging the ball close enough to the floor that your body contact with the floor does not come from a great height.

The most common method of rolling is this: You let the ball drop to approximately a 1-foot height, then hit it high into the air. Contact the floor with your hips and thighs and roll onto your back, bringing your feet and legs over the shoulder on the opposite side of your body from where you hit the ball, and roll back up onto your feet. You can also execute the roll with your feet going over your head or by rolling side to side on your back. You should be capable of rolling to either side. Determine which methods of rolling feel most comfortable (see Figure 16.1).

Figure 16.1 Keys to Success:
Roll

Preparation Phase

1. Move to the ball
2. Low body posture
3. Let the ball drop low

Execution Phase

1. Play ball before contact with floor
2. Play ball toward center of court
3. Two hands are preferred
4. Flick wrists or flex elbows

5. Get ball high
6. Roll quickly to spread force of contact
7. Padded body parts first contact floor

**Follow-Through
Phase**

1. Return to feet quickly
2. Look for ball
3. Prepare for next play

Detecting Roll Errors

There are three major errors in performing the roll: (a) not getting low enough to the floor before digging the ball, (b) attempting to roll before the dig, and (c) contacting the floor with the wrong parts of the body first. It is important that roll errors are corrected as soon as possible because they would most likely cause injury eventually. The style of the roll is no longer of extreme importance as long as these basic errors are corrected.

ERROR

CORRECTION

1. You contact the floor hard, resulting in discomfort.

1. Take a large step toward the ball and assume as low a position as possible.

ERROR

CORRECTION

2. You contact the floor before hitting the ball.

2. You should complete the dig before the roll begins; the roll is a method of recovery.

3. You take too long to return to your feet and are not ready for the next play.

3. Once the roll begins, make the action as quick as possible in order to get back on your feet.

4. You play the ball too high (more than 1 1/2–2 feet) above the floor.

4. The lower you let the ball drop, the better the dig.

Roll
Keys to Success Checklist

If the result of digging and rolling is a ball played high and to the middle of the court so that a teammate can set the attack, the play has been successful. The form of the roll is not critical as long as you prevent yourself from being injured and quickly return to your feet for the execution of the next play.

Have someone check your roll with this checklist.

Preparation
Phase

_____ Digger gets as close to the ball as possible by moving the feet.
_____ Body is in low posture.
_____ Digger allows ball to drop as low as possible, making more time for execution.

Execution
Phase

_____ Ball is contacted before body hits the floor.
_____ Two hands are used whenever possible.

_____ Wrists flick or elbows flex as the ball is dug to aid in getting the ball high.
_____ Roll is quick.
_____ Padded body parts contact the floor.

Follow-Through
Phase

_____ Roller returns to feet as quickly as possible.
_____ Player looks for and finds the ball, to be ready for next play.

HOW TO EXECUTE THE SPRAWL

In a low body position and with your feet in a wide stride, one foot ahead of the other, let the ball drop to about a 1-foot height, reach for the ball, and dig it high to the middle of the court. Continue to move forward, contacting the floor with your arms and chest in a sliding action. Extend your back leg behind you while you bend your front leg at the knee and keep it out to the side, the side of the knee contacting the floor (see Figure 16.2).

It is more difficult to return to your feet after executing a sprawl than after executing a roll. You can make a similar sliding action with your body on its side, particularly after a dig using one hand.

Figure 16.2 Keys to Success: Sprawl

Preparation Phase

1. Take a large step toward ball
2. Wide stride

Execution Phase

1. Play ball low
2. Flick wrists or flex elbows
3. Contact ball before hitting floor
4. Hit ball high

5. Push forward with rear foot
6. Break fall with arms
7. Slide onto chest
8. One knee to the side
9. Extend back leg

**Follow-Through
Phase**

1. Quickly resume defensive position
2. Look for the ball
3. Prepare for next play

d

Detecting Sprawl Errors

With the sprawl, the contact of the ball can be on your forearm, your hand, or the back of your hand. You may use one or both arms, although using two is preferred because it allows for more control. As with the roll, the greatest concern is to play the ball high to the middle of the court in the most efficient manner, while preventing injury.

ERROR

CORRECTION

1. You play the ball at a height greater than 2 feet.

1. Take a big step toward the spot where the ball will be played, at the same time lowering your body.

ERROR CORRECTION

2. You contact the floor before contacting the ball.

2. Contact the ball before the floor so that your hands are available to aid in breaking the fall.

3. You do not rapidly return to your feet.

3. You must quickly return to your feet and assume a low, defensive position.

Sprawl
Keys to Success Checklist

The essential aspect of a good sprawl is the large step toward the ball that allows you to assume a position low to the floor. The closer your body is to the floor, the easier it is to perform the sprawl and the less chance of injury.

Your instructor or another skilled observer should use the criteria below to assess your sprawl.

Preparation
Phase

_____ Feet are in a wide stride, with front foot taking a giant step toward the ball.

Execution
Phase

_____ Digger pushes weight off back foot.
_____ Ball is played in a low position.
_____ Ball is played before contact with the floor.
_____ Flick wrist or flex elbows to aid in getting the ball high to the center of the court.
_____ Eyes stay on the ball until contact.

_____ Arms contact floor first, helping to break force.
_____ Chest hits floor next, sliding in the direction of the ball.
_____ Back leg is extended.
_____ Front leg is bent and to the outside, with contact on the inside of the knee.

Follow-Through
Phase

_____ Player quickly returns to feet.
_____ Player looks for the ball.
_____ Player resumes low defensive position.

Individual Defense Drills

1. Roll Without Ball Drill

Working individually without a ball, practice the rolling skill. Get into a low position, make sure that your padded body parts contact the floor first, and return to your feet as quickly as possible.

Success Goal = complete 10 rolls to either side

Your Score = (#) _____ rolls

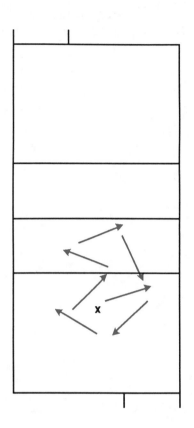

2. Dig to Roll Drill

Have a partner near the net, facing the end line. You stand in the left back position.
   Your partner tosses a low, easy ball alternately to either side of you. Let the ball drop low, dig the ball, and roll, quickly returning to your feet.

Success Goal = a. 5 successful dig-roll combinations out of 10 tosses to the right
   b. 5 successful dig-roll combinations out of 10 tosses to the left

Your Score = a. (#) _____ dig-roll combinations to the right
   b. (#) _____ dig-roll combinations to the left

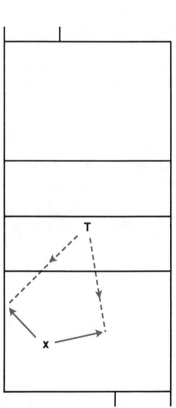

3. Sprawl Without Ball Drill

Working individually, practice the sprawling skill without a ball. Take a large step forward, slide forward as your body contacts the floor, and return to your feet as quickly as possible.

Success Goal = a. 5 sprawls forward
           b. 5 sprawls to the right
           c. 5 sprawls to the left

Your Score = a. (#) _____ sprawls forward
           b. (#) _____ sprawls to the right
           c. (#) _____ sprawls to the left

4. Dig to Sprawl Drill

Stand on the end line in the center back position. Have a partner near the net, facing you.

Your partner tosses a low ball so that it would drop 3–4 feet in front of you. Step forward, reach, and play the ball in a low position, digging it high to the center of the court and sprawling.

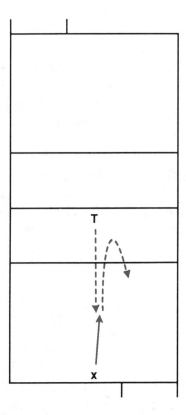

Success Goal = 5 out of 10 successful dig/sprawl combinations

Your Score = (#) _____ dig/sprawl combinations

5. Roll or Sprawl Decision Drill

Stand in any one of the defensive positions on the court. Have a partner stand at the net, facing you.

Your partner tosses the ball to either side, or in front, of you. You must decide which defensive skill to use, dig the ball, and execute the roll or sprawl correctly.

Success Goal = 5 out of 10 correct defensive plays

Your Score = (#) _____ defensive plays

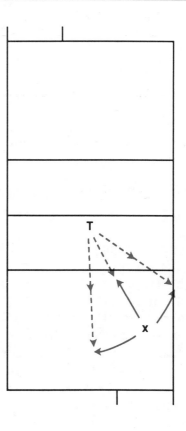

6. Spike Hit, Dig, Sprawl or Roll Drill

Position yourself with a partner as in the previous drill. Your partner tosses the ball to him- or herself and spike hits it at you. Dig the ball higher than the height of the net to the center of the court; use a roll or sprawl when needed. Your partner catches the ball.

Success Goal = 7 out of 10 successful digs

Your Score = (#) _____ digs

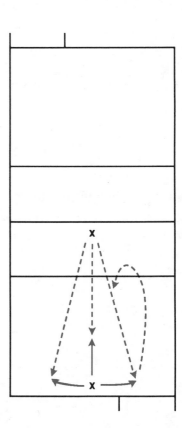

7. Spike, Dig, Roll or Sprawl Drill

Get together a group of four players, two of you on offense and two on defense. On one side of the net, a setter stands close to the net, and a spiker starts at the attack line in the left front position. On the other side, one defensive player is positioned in the center back on the end line; the other defender stands on the left sideline, about 20 feet from the net.

On the offensive side, the setter sets the ball to the spiker, who spikes the ball on the diagonal to the left back quarter of the opponent's side. The defenders both move toward the ball, quickly deciding who should play it. One of them digs the ball, using a roll or sprawl if necessary.

The attackers receive a point for each spike not dug. The defensive players receive a point for each successful dig going higher than the top of the net and to the center of the court.

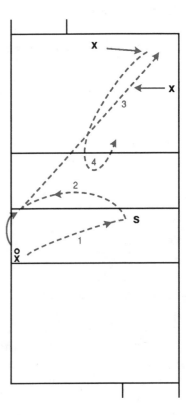

Success Goal = be the first team to reach an agreed-upon number of points

Your Score = (#) _____ team points

Step 17   4–2 Offense

In volleyball, once you master the basic skills and begin to compete in actual game situations, it is necessary to know and use various offensive and defensive strategies. This enhances communication between you and the other players, and helps maintain organized patterns of play. The first strategy that you should learn is the 4–2 offense. The 4–2 offense is considered to be the easiest offense to execute.

Offensive alignments are usually titled numerically, the first number referring to the number of players who primarily serve as attackers and the second number referring to the number of players who serve primarily as setters. Therefore, in the 4–2 offense, four players are attackers and two players are setters.

WHY IS THE 4–2 OFFENSE IMPORTANT?

The 4–2 offense is usually the first offense a team learns. It is called a *simple offense* because the setter is one of the front row players. Only forwards may spike from in front of the attack line; therefore, if one of these players serves as the setter, the team is limited to only two front line attackers. Many teams do not have more than four highly skilled attackers, so these teams find the 4–2 offense more than adequate.

HOW TO EXECUTE THE 4–2 OFFENSE

When examining each offense, this text discusses three areas: serve reception, covering the attacker, and free ball formation. *Serve reception* is when your team is receiving the serve from the opponents. *Covering the attacker* is the action taken to efficiently cover the court during a spike by your team that may be blocked by the opponents. A *free ball formation* is the position taken by your team to receive a ball coming from your opponents that is neither a serve nor a spike. In all three situa-

tions, your team is receiving the ball and is in transition from defense to offense.

Over the years, many serve reception patterns have been introduced into the game. The current thought in this area is that the fewer people assigned to receive the serve, the better the result. Many teams therefore employ two-person, three-person, or four-person serve reception formations. The traditional W-formation remains the most prevalent serve reception pattern at the beginning levels of play. For the purposes of this book, we will concentrate on the W-formation because when it is employed, all players have the opportunity to experience serve reception.

In any serve reception formation, the setter does not want to receive the serve under any circumstances. The setter, therefore, assumes a position either near the net or behind another player (hides).

Until the ball is actually contacted on the serve, all players on *both* teams must be aligned on the court in their correct rotational positions. When offenses and defenses are discussed, you read of rotational positions and playing positions. *Rotational positions* are the positions that players of both teams must be in during the serve. These positions are indicated on the lineup submitted by the coach before the game. *Playing positions* are the positions assumed by players on the court immediately after the serve is executed. Players can assume any position on the court at that time, with the exception that only the forwards may attack or block from in front of the attack line.

Due to the fact that players are allowed to play any position on the court after the serve is initiated, the concept of specialization has become very popular. When a team employs specialization, each player basically plays two positions: one while in the front line and one while in the back line. Because teams rotate each time they gain a side out, players would need to master six different positions on the

172 Volleyball: Steps to Success

court if teams did not specialize. Obviously, specialization facilitates the learning process. When the W-formation for serve reception is diagramed, the players are indicated according to their rotational positions and their functions, for example, attacker or setter, but not according to their specializations.

SERVE RECEPTION

In the 4–2 offense, a setter always sets from the middle of the court close to the net. Two players serve as setters. In the lineup, the setters should be in opposition to one another; that is, left forward and right back, center forward and center back, or right forward and left back. Initially the setters are positioned in the center forward and center back positions. The setter who is the center forward is responsible for the setting duties until rotating into the right back position. At that time, the second setter rotates into the left forward position and assumes the active role of setting. The W-formation is diagramed here for three rotations (see Diagrams 17.1, 17.2, and 17.3). The remaining three rotations repeat the patterns demonstrated in the three diagramed, with the exception that the players will be in opposing positions.

Note that in the diagrams, the setter always "hides" at the net and begins in the correct rotational position. As soon as the serve is contacted, the setter moves to the center front of the court, giving him or her two options for attack—a front set or a back set. The setter always faces the left sideline, having the right foot forward (the foot closer to the net). The setter remains in this position directing the attack until the next serve. When the team is comprised of all right-handed players, the left side of the court is the strong side because the left forward is attacking on-hand.

In Diagram 17.1, the setter is the center forward and no switch is necessry. In Diagrams 17.2 and 17.3, the setter must switch from an outside position to the center of the court. In each of these last two cases, the center forward attacker is in position on the same side of the court as the setter and is preparing to become an outside attacker.

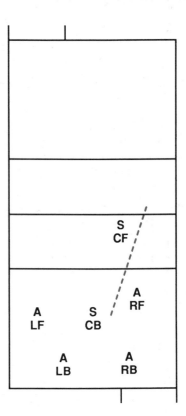

Diagram 17.1 W-formation, serve reception, 4–2 offense, setter in the CF position.

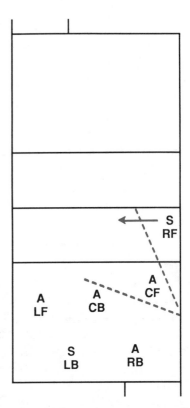

Diagram 17.2 W-formation, serve reception, 4–2 offense, setter in the RF position.

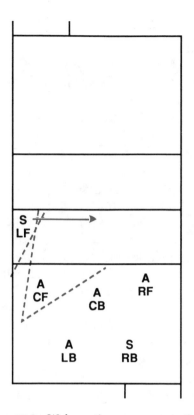

Diagram 17.3   W-formation, serve reception, 4–2 offense, setter in the LF position.

right and left back players function as a team, helping each other call "out" on any ball that is long; one player calls for the ball, and the second watches to see whether they should call it out. The left forward with the left back, and the right forward with the right back act as teams to call the left sideline and the right sideline. When any player calls for the ball, the matched player decides whether the serve is good or out-of-bounds. Any "watcher" must call "out" as soon as possible, so that the receiver does not attempt to play the ball.

When receiving serve, your team is attempting to gain a side out. Serve reception is a total team effort and requires concentration and communication. If only one member of the team does not assume the responsibility given, the entire team may fail.

Diagram 17.4 indicates the areas of responsibility for each of the five players during serve reception.

Teams must be aware of the potential for overlap in these two alignments. Lines are drawn in the diagrams to indicate the problem areas of overlap (Diagrams 17.2 and 17.3). The center back must remain behind the center forward, and the setter must be sure to remain closer to the sideline than the center forward when the ball is served.

In order to receive serve efficiently, a team must utilize certain guidelines. The back line players always position themselves so that they have a clear view of the server as they look between the front line players. The player receiving serve must call for the ball before the ball crosses the plane of the net. All players must turn and face the player who has called for the ball; this action is referred to as *opening up* to the ball. No players should receive any serve that is chest high or above; the front row players should allow the back row players to receive this serve, and the back row players should allow this serve to go out.

The setter and center back players should signal their teammates if a serve is short. The

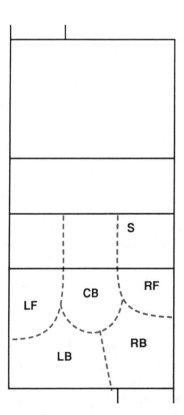

Diagram 17.4   Areas of serve-reception responsibility for all players when using the W-formation.

RULE SUMMARY FOR SUCCESSFUL SERVE RECEPTION

All Players

- decide who will receive the ball as soon as possible after contact by the server,
- call for the ball before it crosses the plane of the net,
- open up to the player playing the ball, and
- help call the ball out-of-bounds for other players.

Front Row Players

- allow balls that are higher than chest level to be played by back row players,
- do not move back more than one step to play the ball,
- call the ball out on the sideline for the back row player on the same side of the court, and
- are ready to move forward quickly on short serves.

Back Row Players

- allow a ball that is at chest height or higher to go out-of-bounds,
- call the ball out on the sideline for the front row player on the same side of the court,
- are more aggressive from the left back position in receiving when the ball is between the left and right backs,
- call the ball out over the end line for the other back, and
- always position themselves between the front row players.

Setters

- never receive the serve,
- call short serves,
- call for the pass and extend the hand closer to the net high as a target for the passer, and
- face the left sideline with the right foot forward in the stride position.

COVERING THE ATTACKER

Once your team has received the serve and has passed to the setter, you attempt to complete an offensive attack. Meanwhile, the opposing team is attempting to prevent your team from completing a successful attack. Your team must be ready and cover the court regardless of the result of your attack. There are five possible outcomes of every attack. In three of these outcomes, the ball becomes dead and play is completed. The results that end in a dead ball are (a) the attacker spikes the ball to the floor for a point, (b) the attacker spikes the ball out-of-bounds or makes an error, or (c) the blocker blocks the ball out-of-bounds or makes an error.

In the fourth and fifth attack outcomes, the ball remains in play. Either the defensive team digs the ball and prepares for a counterattack, or the blocker(s) successfully blocks the ball and it remains on your side of the court. If the opposing block is successful, the ball remains in play, falling quickly to the floor in an area directly behind the attacker. Therefore, this is the critical area for your team to cover.

In the 3–2 coverage, three of your players make a semicircle behind the attacker, while the remaining two players position themselves in the spaces between them (see Diagrams 17.5 and 17.6). The person closest to the sideline is the back row player on the same side of the court as the attacker. The person in the middle of the three is *always* the center back. The player closest to the net is always the setter, who sets the attacker and follows the set by moving to the coverage position. These three players must be in a low defensive position to have as much time as possible to react to the ball. They must be low in position when the ball is contacted by the opposing spiker.

The two offensive players toward the sideline opposite the attacker's side shift toward the attack side and align themselves in the spaces between the three-player semicircle. Diagram 17.5 illustrates the 3–2 coverage when your left forward is attacking. Diagram 17.6 illustrates the 3–2 coverage when your right forward is attacking.

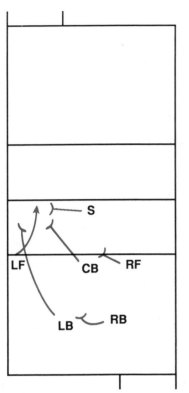

Diagram 17.5 Spike coverage when your LF is spiking.

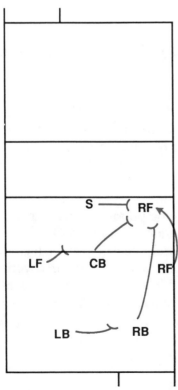

Diagram 17.6 Spike coverage when your RF is spiking.

If the ball goes by or is deflected by the block and is dug by the defense, your team must quickly assume the base defensive formation. This formation will be covered during the discussion of defense.

FREE BALL

Any time the opposing team is playing the ball and attempting to set its attack, your team's blockers are at the net anticipating their next action to be a block. When it becomes obvious that the opposing team does not have enough control to complete their attack, your team must prepare to receive a free ball. Lack of control is often indicated when the first pass does not go toward the net, when a player other than the setter must handle the second ball, when the set is made to a distance of more than 10 feet off the net, or when the attacker is out of position.

The free ball formation is very similar to the W-formation. The only difference is the setter is already in position at the center front of the court. The setter usually calls "free" to communicate with the team that no block is necessary. Your team should immediately move to free ball formation. The setter remains at the net, the two attackers move straight back to the attack line, and the center back moves close to the attack line at the center of the court. The remaining two backs fill in the spaces in between the forwards.

The attackers' first priority is to receive the ball; their second priority is to prepare to attack. As soon as the two attackers are sure that they will not have to receive the free ball, they move to the sidelines of the court and prepare to receive the set. It is critical that the attackers do not "wing out" like this (see Diagram 17.7) until they are positive that the free ball will be passed by a teammate. The number 1 on the diagram indicates the direction of the attackers' first movement straight back to the attack line. The number 2 on the diagram is the wing out, or second movement by the attacker to a position outside the sidelines in preparation for the attack. Once the free ball is received, your team sets its own attack and proceeds with appropriate coverage.

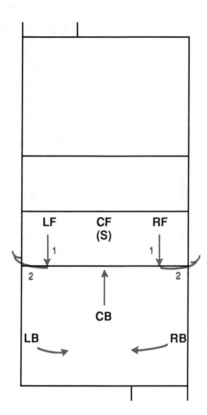

Diagram 17.7 Movement from base defense to free
ball.

Detecting 4–2 Offense Errors

Errors in the execution of the 4–2 offense can
be categorized into three main areas: (a) not
assuming the position indicated by the play
situation; (b) moving toward the correct position, but not arriving at that spot soon
enough; and (c) assuming the correct position,
but executing poorly. Errors in all three offensive formations—serve reception, covering the
attacker, and free ball—can be included in the
first category above. Errors in covering the attacker and free ball are more frequently found
in the second category. Serve reception errors
are most commonly of the type found in
category three.

ERROR 🚫

CORRECTION

1. The setter receives the serve.

1. Setter should "hide" at the net and not receive the serve under any circumstances.

2. A free ball falls between a front row player and a back row player.

2. The two forwards must move off the net to the attack line as quickly as possible and assume a ready position prior to the opponent making contact with the ball that is being sent over the net.

3. The ball rebounds off the opponent's block and falls to the floor on the attacker's side.

3. Three players must assume a coverage position around the attacker.

4. A player in the W-formation gets hit on the back by a passed ball.

4. All players must open up to the receiver by turning and facing that player.

5. The serve falls to the court between two players.

5. Receivers must call for the serve prior to the ball's crossing the net.

6. The ball rebounds off the block and falls to the court between the coverage and the sideline.

6. The player covering closest to the line should have the outside foot on the sideline and should not play any ball that rebounds off the block beyond the sideline side of the body.

7. The attacker prevents the coverage from playing the ball.

7. The attacker should not play a ball that rebounds off the block, unless it stays between the attacker and the net.

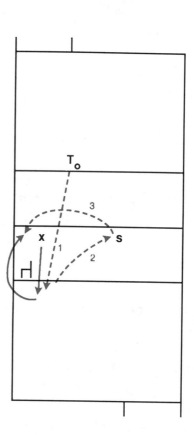

1. Wing Out Drill

Place a chair at the attack line at the left side-line. You need two partners for this drill. One is a setter, positioned at the net in the middle of the court. You are a left forward in blocking position on the same side of the court as the chair. Your other partner is a tosser on the opposite side of the net.

The tosser yells ''free'' and tosses the ball high and easy to the attack line. You, the left forward, move straight back to the attack line, overhead pass the ball to the setter, ''wing out'' around the chair, and approach to complete an attack. The setter sets a high, outside set. Repeat this drill on the right side of the court.

Success Goal = a. 8 out of 10 successful attacks from the left forward position
b. 7 out of 10 successful attacks from the right forward position

Your Score = a. (#) _____ attacks from the left forward position
b. (#) _____ attacks from the right forward position

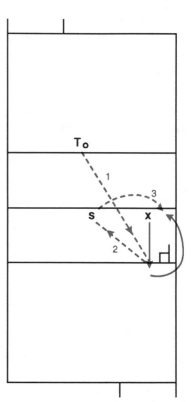

2. Serve Receive Drill

A team of six lines up on one side of the court. A server on the opposite side of the court serves the ball underhand to the receiving team. The team goes into a W-formation with the setter in the center forward position. The team receives the serve, executes an attack either forward or back, and covers the attacker correctly.

The team receives 5 good serves, then rotates one position. Continue this drill until all players have rotated all the way around to the original starting positions.

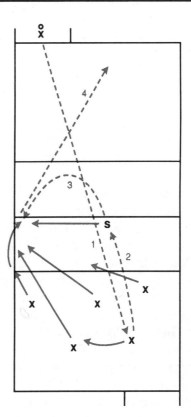

Success Goal = 24 out of 30 successful attacks with the correct coverage

Your Score = (#) _____ attacks with the correct coverage

3. Free Ball Drill

A team of six lines up on one side of the court, with the three forwards at the net in blocking position. The center back is in the center of the court, and the left and right backs are on their respective sidelines 20 feet from the net. A tosser is on the opposite side of the net.

The tosser yells "free," delays for a couple of seconds, then tosses the ball over the net high and easy. The team of six quickly moves into the W-formation. They receive the ball, set an attack, and cover the attacker.

The team receives 5 balls, then rotates one position. Continue this drill until the players have rotated to their original starting positions.

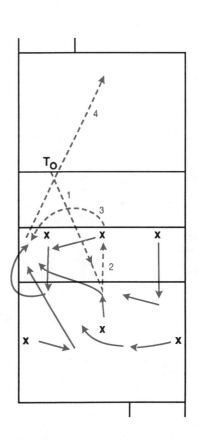

Success Goal = 24 out of 30 successful attacks with the proper coverage

Your Score = (#) _____ successful attacks with the proper coverage

4. Cover and Dig Drill

A team of six stands on one side of the court in the same starting positions as in the Free Ball Drill (see Drill 3). Two blockers stand on a box on the right side of the court on the opposite side of the net.

A tosser on the same court as the blockers yells "free" and throws a high ball over the net. The team receives the free ball, sets the attack to their left forward, and covers. The blockers block the ball. The attacking coverage attempts to set up with a successful dig—a dig that initiates a second completed attack.

The team receives 5 tosses, then rotates one position. Continue the drill until players have returned to their original positions.

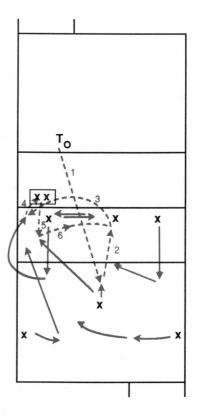

Success Goal = 18 out of 30 successful digs off the opposing block

Your Score = (#) _____ digs off the opposing block

5. Serve and Free Ball Drill

Have a team of six on one side of the net, and a tosser and a server each with a ball on the opposite side. The server serves. The receiving team, positioned in the W-formation, receives serve, sets the attack, and covers.

Then the team immediately assumes starting positions as in the Free Ball Drill (see Drill 3). The opposing tosser calls "free" and tosses a ball high over the net. The receiving team passes the free ball, sets an attack, and covers. Play continues with another serve and attack immediately followed by another free ball.

The team receives 5 good serves, then rotates one position. The drill continues until all players return to their starting positions.

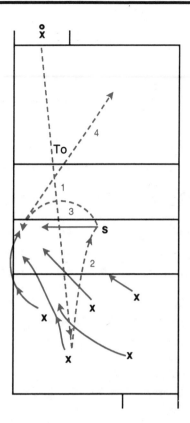

Success Goal = a. 24 out of 30 successful attacks off serve receives
  b. 24 out of 30 successful attacks off free balls

Your Score = a. (#) _____ attacks off serve receives
  b. (#) _____ attacks off free balls

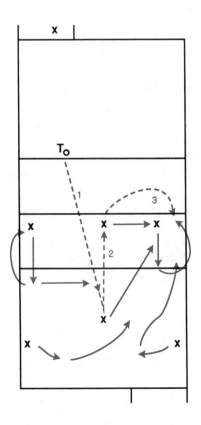

Step 18 2–1–3 Defense

When the ball goes over the net to the opposing team, your team should immediately move to the base defensive formation. This formation is used until the type of ball to be returned from the opponent becomes evident; the two possible plays are either a free ball or an attack. The free ball formation was described in Step 17.

When the opposing team executes an attack, the most effective way of defending it is with a block and backcourt coverage. In the 2–1–3 defense, the 2 represents the blockers, the 1 is a player who is positioned behind the block, and the 3 indicates the backcourt players. When using the 2–1–3 defense, the team assumes that the block will protect at least the deep area of the court behind it. The off-blocker and backcourt players must be strategically positioned to cover the remaining court.

WHY IS THE 2–1–3 DEFENSE IMPORTANT?

When your opponents are playing the ball, your team wishes to be in the most advantageous position to react quickly when the ball is returned to your side of the court. An attack takes very little time to travel from the hitter's hand to the floor; therefore, you must be in a position such that your primary action is reacting to the ball without having to cover much ground. The base defensive formation places the blockers close to the net, ready to block, and the backcourt players close to those court areas they will cover behind the block.

The strength of the 2–1–3 defensive formation is that it affords good protection against a team that makes use of many off-speed attacks and dinks. The player behind the block is in position to receive these types of attack easily. In order to be successful in using the 2–1–3, a team must have strong blocking. If

the block is weak, a large portion of the court behind the block is very vulnerable. Another important aspect of this defense is that each backcourt player is generally responsible for receiving only one type of attack, either a hard-driven spike, or a soft attack (off-speed spike, or a dink). This makes his or her role easier.

HOW TO EXECUTE THE 2–1–3 DEFENSE

The 2–1–3 defensive formation is usually the first defensive system learned by beginning teams. Because each player has the responsibility of receiving only one type of attack, the roles are clearly defined and easier to execute. This defense is also strong against other beginning teams because at this level the opponents are more likely to use off-speed attacks and dinks than hard-driven spikes.

BASE

When using the 2–1–3 defense in the base formation, the center back player remains in the middle of the court. The two attackers and the setter stay at the net, anticipating a block. The remaining two defensive players position themselves 20 feet from the net and close to their respective sidelines (see Diagram 18.1).

The base defensive position is held until a team leader determines whether the team should block or move into a free ball formation. It is extremely important that all players on the team move into the same formation. Even if the team leader errs and calls ''free ball'' only to have the opposing team attack, if everyone is in the same formation, the team is still capable of receiving the ball. If, however, some players block and others move to free ball, there will exist open areas on the court that will be very vulnerable. Diagram 18.2 shows base defense to free ball formation.

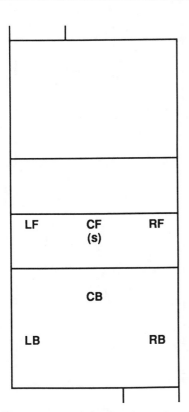

Diagram 18.1 Base defensive formation for the 2–1–3 defense.

BLOCK

If the opponents spike, your team should attempt to block; you must align yourselves behind the block in the most strategic manner. Your team should execute a double block against each spike attempt. The outside blocker decides where to set the block. The blocker should line up half of a body width to the attacker's hitting side. The middle blocker moves to the outside blocker and joins to make a double block. The blockers' hands must be far enough apart to protect as much court area as possible, yet close enough together to prevent the ball from going through the block. The outside blocker's responsibility is the ball. The middle blocker is responsible for the angle.

Once the block is formed, the remaining four players move to positions to cover those parts of the court not protected by the block. Diagram 18.3 indicates the movement of players from the base defensive formation to a blocking formation using the 2–1–3 alignment against an attack from the opposing right forward.

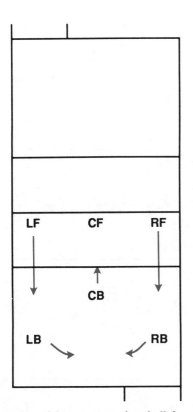

Diagram 18.2 Movement to free ball from base defensive formation.

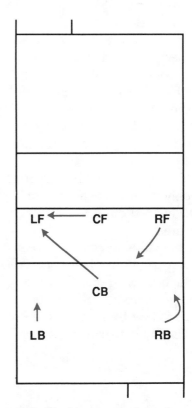

Diagram 18.3 Blocking an attack by the opposing RF, using the 2–1–3 defense.

The center forward joins the left forward to form the block. The off-blocker, the right forward, drops off the net to the attack line and moves into the court around 10 feet. The off-blocker's responsibilities are handling sharp-angled spikes toward the sideline, dinks to the middle of the court close to the net, and "junk" off the net (balls that hit the top of the net, roll, and fall to the court).

The right back is in the part of the court referred to as the *power alley* because any spike that passes the block is very likely to go into this area. The right back lines up with his or her back to the sideline and with a line of view to the ball along the center forward's inside shoulder and the attacker's hand. The center back moves to a position immediately behind, and to the middle of, the block in a low defensive posture. The center back's responsibility is any off-speed spike or dink directed over the block, down-the-line, or to the center of the court. The left back is positioned on the sideline 20 feet from the net and has the responsibility to receive any attacks directed down-the-line.

Diagrams 18.4 and 18.5 show the movement of players when defending against an opposing attack from the center forward and left forward, respectively. Note that when the opposing center forward is attacking, the team is using a single blocker and both off-blockers move to the attack line to play defensive roles. This attack is usually a quick attack; the outside blockers find it difficult to have enough time to join the center forward to form a double or a triple block. The responsibilities of each player on defense are similar for all positions, even though the attack is from a different area.

When the ball is directed between two defensive players, both players move laterally toward the ball, with the player closer to the net crossing in front of the deeper player. If all players follow this concept, there should be no collisions between them (see Diagram 18.6).

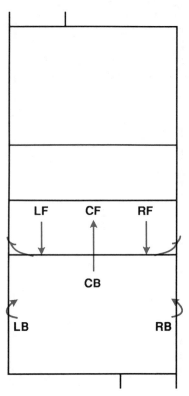

Diagram 18.4 Blocking an attack by the opposing CF, using the 2–1–3 defense.

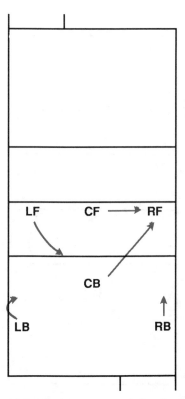

Diagram 18.5 Blocking an attack by the opposing LF, using the 2–1–3 defense.

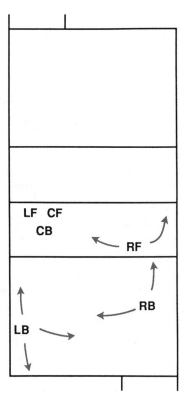

Diagram 18.6 Player movement to dig attacks directed between two players.

RULE SUMMARY FOR SUCCESSFUL BLOCK DEFENSE

All Players

- should anticipate play of opponents by attempting to read what the opponents will do, and
- move to the defensive position, set, and be ready to react before the ball is contacted by the attacker.

Front Row Players

- should have hands at shoulder level or higher in starting position,
- should move along the net left and right but never away from the net and back to the net,
- should have no arm swing,
- must penetrate the net with hands on the block, and
- when playing the off-blocker, move to the attack line ready to play defense.

Back Court Players

- keep low body posture with weight forward on the toes, and
- move through the ball toward the target.

Off-Blocker

- plays dinks to the center of the court and close to the net,
- plays junk off the net—any ball that rolls along the top of the net and falls into the court area, and
- plays hard-driven spikes at the sharp angle to the sideline.

Center Back

- plays in a low posture behind the block, ready to receive dinks over the block.

Defensive Players on Line

- must play any spike down-the-line.

Power Alley Player

- aligns so that the inside shoulder of the middle blocker, the ball, and the attacker's hand are all in view, and
- receives spikes or off-speeds into the power alley.

Detecting 2–1–3 Defense Errors

When discussing errors in the execution of the 2–1–3 defense, we are mainly emphasizing the incorrect position of players. In defending an opposing attack, the defensive alignment has to be ready in a set initial position by the time the ball is contacted by the attacker. The ability of players to read the actions of the opponents greatly enhances defensive success. This ability allows players to move into the correct initial position efficiently. Once in position, the backcourt players must have a low body posture with their weight forward.

ERROR

CORRECTION

ERROR	CORRECTION
1. The ball goes through the block.	1. The middle blocker must close the block.
2. The attacker hits successfully down the line.	2. The right or left backs must stay on the line when defending deep behind the block.
3. An attacker successfully dinks over the block.	3. The center back must move into a position behind and close to the block.
4. The ball rebounds off the player in the power alley and continues out-of-bounds.	4. The power alley players—the left back and right back—position themselves with their backs to the sidelines so that the spike is in front of them.
5. The ball goes off the blockers' hands and out-of-bounds.	5. The outside blocker should turn the hand closer to the sideline in toward the court to keep the ball inbounds.

2–1–3 Defense Drills

1. Digging a Dink: Left Forward Attacker Drill

On one side of the net, there is a setter and an attacker in the left forward position. On the opposite side, there are three blockers and a center back.

The attacker tosses the ball to the setter, who sets the ball back to the attacker. The attacker dinks the ball over the block, either down-the-line or to the center of the court. The center back covers dinks down-the-line, and the off-blocker covers dinks to the center of the court.

Success Goal = a. on defense, successfully digging 8 out of 10 dinks
b. on offense, successfully dinking 10 out of 12 sets

Your Score = a. (#) _____ dinks dug
b. (#) _____ dinks executed

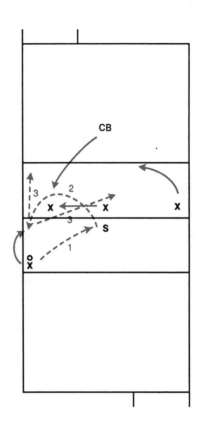

2. Digging a Dink: Right Forward Attacker Drill

This is the same as the previous drill, with the exception that the attacker is in the right forward position. Another player is needed to toss the ball to the setter, who back sets to the attacker.

Success Goal = a. on defense, successfully digging 8 out of 10 dinks
b. on offense, successfully dinking 10 out of 12 sets

Your Score = a. (#) _____ dinks dug
b. (#) _____ dinks executed

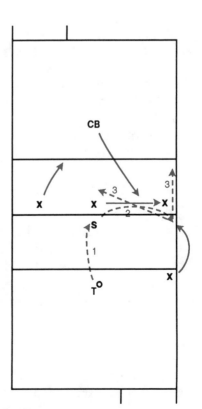

3. *Digging Down-the-Line Spikes: Right Back Drill*

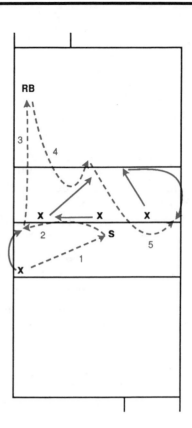

On one side of the net, there are three blockers and a right back defending the line. On the opposite side, there are a left forward and a setter.

The attacker tosses the ball to the setter, who sets high and outside. The blockers give the attacker the line (they line up to block only the angle). The attacker spikes the ball down-the-line. The right back digs the ball high to the center of the court, and the center forward sets an attack.

Success Goal = a. 10 out of 12 down-the-line spikes by the attacker
b. 6 out of 10 successful digs by the right back
c. 4 out of 6 completed attacks on the transition

Your Score = a. (#) _____ down-the-line spikes
b. (#) _____ digs
c. (#) _____ completed attacks on the transition

4. *Digging Down-the-Line Spikes: Left Back Drill*

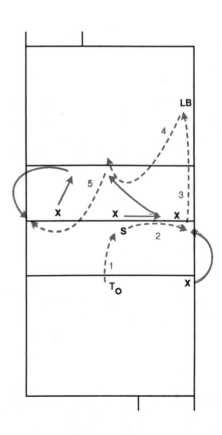

This is the same as the previous drill, with the exception that the attacker is in the right forward position, and the left back digs the spiked balls. Another player should toss the ball to the setter, who back sets to the attacker.

Success Goal = a. 10 out of 12 down-the-line spikes by the attacker
b. 6 out of 10 successful digs by the left back
c. 4 out of 6 completed attacks on the transition

Your Score = a. (#) _____ down-the-line spikes
b. (#) _____ digs
c. (#) _____ completed attacks on the transition

5. Digging Cross-Court: Left Back Drill

On one side of the net, there are three blockers and a left back defensive player. On the opposite court, there are a setter and an attacker in the left forward position.

The attacker tosses the ball to the setter, who sets high and outside. The attacker spikes cross-court. The left back or off-blocker digs the ball, and the forwards attempt to complete an attack on transition.

Success Goal = a. 10 out of 12 successful attacks
b. 6 out of 10 successful digs
c. 4 out of 6 completed attacks on the transition

Your Score = a. (#) _____ cross-court spikes
b. (#) _____ digs
c. (#) _____ attacks on the transition

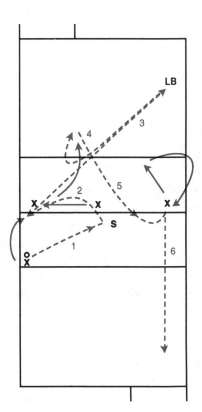

6. Digging Cross-Court: Right Back Drill

This is the same as the previous drill, with the exception that the attacker is in the right forward position and the defensive player is in the right back position. An additional player is used to toss the ball to the setter, who back sets to the attacker.

Success Goal = a. 10 out of 12 successful attacks
b. 6 out of 10 successful digs
c. 4 out of 6 completed attacks on the transition

Your Score = a. (#) _____ attacks
b. (#) _____ digs
c. (#) _____ attacks on the transition

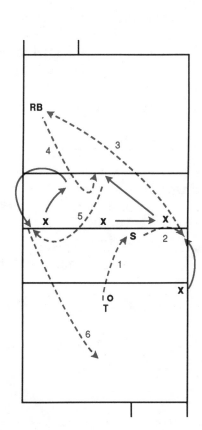

7. Attack and Counterattack Drill

A team of six on one side of the court sets up in base defensive position. A tosser, setter, and two attackers are on the opposite side.

The tosser overhand tosses the ball to the setter, who sets either attacker, permitting him or her to spike over the net. The defending team must block the spike, or receive it and attempt to execute a counterattack. If the attacking players are unable to spike, the defending team should move to a free ball position to receive the third hit over. When the team executes the attack, they must cover the attacker.

The defending team should complete successful counterattacks, then rotate one position. Continue this drill until the players have rotated back to their original positions.

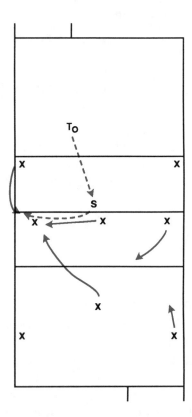

Success Goal = a. 10 out of 12 successful attacks
    b. 6 out of 10 successful digs and completed attacks on transition

Your Score = a. (#) _____ spikes
    b. (#) _____ digs with attacks on transition

Step 19   International 4–2

The International 4–2 offense is similar to the regular 4–2 offense in that four players function primarily as attackers and two players are primarily setters. The difference between the International 4–2 and the regular 4–2 is the position the setter takes at the net. In the regular 4–2, the setter assumes the center forward position. In the International 4–2, the setter assumes the right forward position. In this introduction of the International 4–2, only the implications of this difference will be discussed.

WHY IS THE INTERNATIONAL 4–2 IMPORTANT?

Many teams prefer the International 4–2 over the regular 4–2 because the location of the setter (right forward position) means that both attackers, if right-handed, are hitting on-hand. This implies that the team is attacking from the most powerful position. A disadvantage of the International 4–2 comes when your setter is small in stature, because the setup dictates that the setter block the opponent's strong side attacker.

EXECUTION OF THE INTERNATIONAL 4–2

The International 4–2 is similar to the regular 4–2; therefore, your team should find it easy to move from one to the other. Seeing that there are attackers in the left forward and center forward positions, your team can become accustomed to using a middle attack. This prepares you for advancing to a multiple offense.

SERVE RECEPTION

Serve reception formation for the International 4–2 is close to the W-formation described in Step 17. The only differences are based upon the location of the setter. The setters begin in the right forward and left back positions. In the initial W-formation, no switch by the setter is necessary. It is the right back who moves toward the attack line and appears to be a forward line player as illustrated in Diagram 19.1.

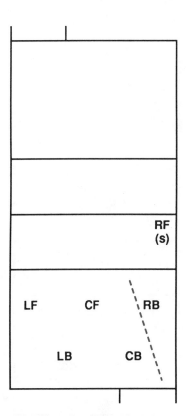

Diagram 19.1 Serve reception when setter is RF, using the International 4–2.

In Diagrams 19.2 and 19.3, the setter must switch from the rotational position to the playing position. The two attackers always receive on the left side and in the middle of the court, shifting to these positions depending on where the setter is located. The right back always adjusts to the right forward position. On the diagrams, the broken line indicates where there is a danger of overlapping. Diagram 19.4 shows the areas of responsibility for all players.

RULE SUMMARY FOR SUCCESSFUL SERVE RECEPTION

All Players

- decide who will receive the ball as soon as possible after contact by the server,
- call for the ball before it crosses the plane of the net,
- open up to the player playing the ball, and
- help call the ball out-of-bounds for other players.

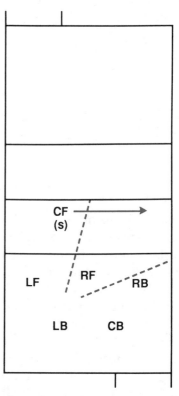

Diagram 19.3   Serve reception when setter is CF, using the International 4–2.

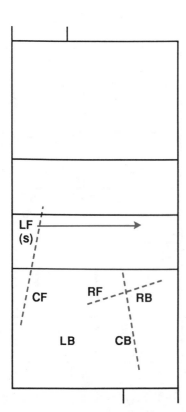

Diagram 19.2   Serve reception when setter is LF, using the International 4–2.

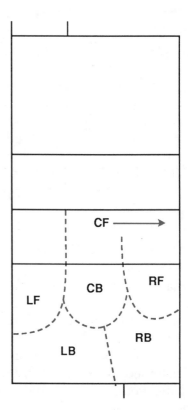

Diagram 19.4   Serve-reception responsibilities, W-formation, International 4–2.

Front Row Players

- allow balls that are higher than chest level to be played by back row players,
- do not move back more than one step to play the ball,
- call the ball out on the sideline for the back row player on the same side of the court, and
- are ready to move forward quickly on short serves.

Back Row Players

- allow a ball that is at chest height or higher to go out-of-bounds,
- call the ball out on the sideline for the front row player on the same side of the court,
- are more aggressive from the left back position in receiving it when the ball is between the left and right backs,
- call the ball out over the end line for each other, and
- always position themselves between the front row players.

Setters

- never receive a serve,
- call short serves,
- call for the pass and extend hand closer to the net high as a target for the passer, and
- face the left sideline with the right foot forward in the stride position.

COVERING THE ATTACKER

In the International 4–2, the coverage of the attacker is similar to that used in the regular 4–2. The same 3–2 formation is used, that is, three people form a semicircle around the attacker, and the remaining two players shift and fill the spaces between those three. The differences are in which players assume which positions in the formation and that the two attackers are now coming from the center forward and left forward positions rather than the left forward and right forward positions.

Refer to Diagrams 19.5 and 19.6 for the proper coverage in the International 4–2.

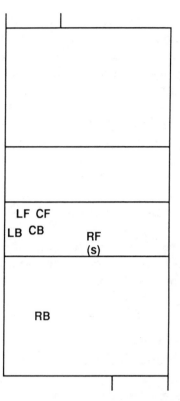

Diagram 19.5   Spike coverage, LF spiking, International 4–2.

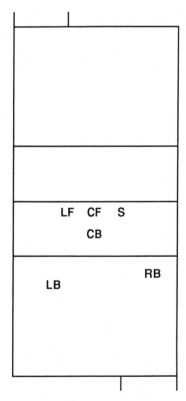

Diagram 19.6   Spike coverage, CF spiking, International 4–2.

When the attacker is the left forward, the left back, center back, and right back are in the same positions and have the same responsibilities as in the regular 4–2. The center forward and right forward are also in the same positions, but the center forward is now an attacker, and the right forward the setter; this is reversed from the alignment in the regular 4–2. In the coverage for an attack by the center forward, the left forward, center back, and setter (right forward) form the semicircle around the attacker, while the left back and the right back align themselves in the spaces between those three players. The basis for the 3–2 coverage is always the same though: Three players form the semicircle around the attacker, and two players fill the spaces.

FREE BALL

In the International 4–2, the free ball formation is the same W as used in the regular 4–2. The difference is that the setter is the right forward. This implies that the two attackers moving off the net are now in the left forward and center forward positions, the setter remains at the net, the right back must move forward into what appears to be a front line position, and the center back must move right and fill the right point of the W. Diagram 19.7 illustrates the movement of the players from base defense to free ball position in the International 4–2.

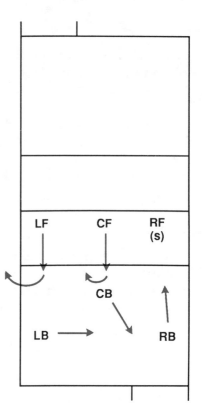

Diagram 19.7 Base defense to free ball, International 4–2.

Detecting International 4–2 Offense Errors

Errors made when using the International 4–2 are very similar to those indicated with the regular 4–2. The main difference is in the location and movement of the setter and the right back player. The setter's playing position is right forward. The right back is the player who adjusts position depending on where the setter is located. Often it is the failure of the right back to make this adjustment that causes errors.

ERROR ⊘	CORRECTION
1. The setter receives the serve.	1. Setter should hide at the net and not receive the serve under any circumstances.
2. A free ball falls between a front row player and a back row player.	2. The two forwards must move off the net to the attack line as quickly as possible and assume a ready position prior to the opponent making contact with the ball to send it over the net.
3. The ball rebounds off the opponent's block and falls to the floor on the attacker's side.	3. Three players must assume a coverage position around the attacker.
4. A player in the W-formation gets hit on the back by a passed ball.	4. All players must open up to the receiver by turning and facing that player.
5. The serve falls to the court between two players.	5. Receivers must call for the serve prior to the ball's crossing the net.
6. The ball rebounds off the block and falls to the court between the coverage and the sideline.	6. The player covering closest to the line should have the outside foot on the sideline and should not play a ball that rebounds off the block beyond the sideline side of the body.
7. The attacker prevents the coverage from playing the ball.	7. The attacker should not play a ball that rebounds off the block, unless it stays between the attacker and the net.
8. A free ball falls to the court in the right forward position.	8. The setter is the right forward and remains at the net; therefore, the right back must adjust and cover this area of the court.
9. The setter attempts to back set.	9. The two eligible attackers are in the center forward and left forward positions; there is no right forward attacker to whom to back set.

International 4–2 Offense Drills

1. Wing Out Drill

Place a chair at the attack line at the left sideline. Have a partner be a setter at the net on the right side of the court. You be a left forward in blocking position on the same side of the court as the chair.

Another partner, on the opposite side of the net, yells "free" and tosses the ball high and easy to the attack line. You, the left forward, move straight back to the attack line, overhead pass the ball to the setter, wing out around the chair, and approach for an attack. The setter sets a high, outside set. Attack. The drill is repeated with you as center forward in the center of the court.

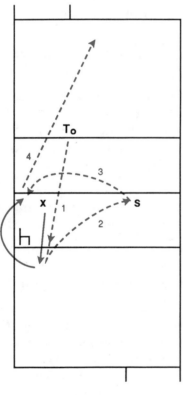

Attack by left forward

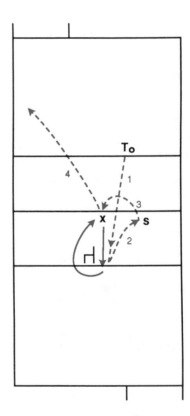

Attack by center forward

Success Goal = a. 8 out of 10 successful attacks from the left forward position
b. 8 out of 10 successful attacks from the center forward position

Your Score = a. (#) _____ attacks from the left forward position
b. (#) _____ attacks from the center forward position

2. Serve Receive Drill

A team of six lines up on one side of the court, with a server on the opposite side of the court.

The server serves the ball underhand to the receiving team. Using the W-formation with the setter in the right forward position, the team receives the serve, executes an attack by either the left or center forward, and covers the attacker.

The team receives 5 good serves, then rotates one position. Continue this drill until the players have rotated around to their original starting positions.

Success Goal = 24 out of 30 successful attacks with the correct coverage

Your Score = (#) _____ attacks

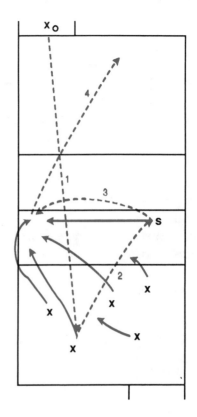

3. Free Ball Drill

A team of six lines up on one side of the court with the three forwards at the net in blocking position. The center back is in the center of the court, and the left and right backs are on their respective sidelines 20 feet from the net. A tosser is on the court on the opposite side of the net.

The tosser yells "free," delays for a couple of seconds, then tosses the ball over the net high and easy. The team of six quickly moves into the W-formation, receives the ball, sets an attack, and covers the attacker. The right back must move forward to fill the position not filled by the setter, who must remain at the net. The center back adjusts to the right back's area of the court.

The team receives 5 balls, then rotates one position. Continue this drill until the players have rotated around to their original starting positions.

Success Goal = 24 out of 30 successful attacks with the proper coverage

Your Score = (#) _____ attacks

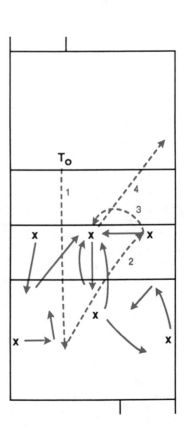

4. Cover and Dig Drill

A team of six sets up on one side of the court in the same starting positions as in the Serve Receive Drill. Two blockers stand on a box on the right side of the court on the opposite side of the net.

A tosser on the same court as the blockers yells "free" and throws a high ball over the net. The team receives the free ball, sets the attack to their left forward, and covers. The blockers block the ball, and the coverage digs successfully to set up for a second attack.

The team receives 5 tosses, then rotates one position. Continue this drill until the players have rotated around to their original positions.

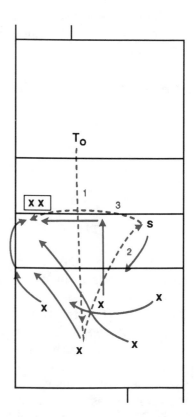

Success Goal = 18 out of 30 successful digs off the opposing block

Your Score = (#) _____ digs

5. *Serve and Free Ball Drill*

A team of six sets up in the W-formation. A tosser and a server are on the opposite side of the net, each with a volleyball. The server serves. The receiving team sets, attacks, and covers.

The team immediately assumes starting positions as in Free Ball Drill (see Drill 3). The tosser calls "free" and tosses the ball high over the net. The receiving team passes the free ball, sets an attack, and covers.

Play continues with another serve, immediately followed by another free ball, and so on. The team receives 5 good serve-free ball sequences and rotates one position. Continue the drill until the players rotate around to their starting positions.

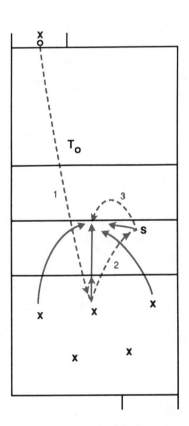

Attack off serve reception

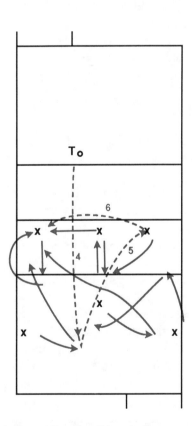

Attack off free ball

Success Goal = a. 24 out of 30 successful attacks off serves
b. 24 out of 30 successful attacks off free balls

Your Score = a. (#) _____ attacks off serves
b. (#) _____ attacks off free balls

Step 20 **6–2 Offense**

The 6–2 volleyball offense is a more powerful offense than either the 4–2 or the International 4–2. The main reason for this is that the setter is a back row player, which allows a team to attack from all three forward positions—left, center, and right. The two setters are still opposite each other in the lineup. The setter in the back row performs the setting duties, whereas the setter in the front row is an attacker. All six players attack, and two players have the primary responsibility of setting. The 6–2 is considered a multiple offense because the setter penetrates to the net from the back row. This characteristic is indicative of all multiple offenses.

WHY IS THE 6–2 OFFENSE IMPORTANT?

The 6–2 offense is important because it allows a team an additional option for their attack. This means that teams can formulate and run a system of plays that includes various combinations of players and movement of players to different parts of the net. This concept of developing a system of plays is very advanced and beyond the scope of this book. Most of these combination plays are based on the ability of the middle attacker to hit a quick set. A quick set is set immediately in front of the setter and only approximately 1 foot above the top of the net. Teams selecting the 6–2 offense must have at least six players who are efficient attackers.

HOW TO EXECUTE THE 6–2 OFFENSE

The main differences between the serve receive W-formation for the simple offenses and for the multiple offenses involve two players. The setter is a back row player and does not receive serve, while all three front row players are involved in serve reception. The center back player receives serve in the deep court rather than in the front court (Diagram 20.1).

SERVE RECEPTION

The W-formation for serve reception can be used with the 6–2. The setter is a back row player and, therefore, must initially hide behind a front row player rather than in a position close to the net. When the setter is the right back or center back player, the movement to the net is rather easy because the distance is short. However, when the setter is in the left back position, the movement is fairly difficult because the distance is rather long. It is extremely important that the setter initiates movement to the net the instant the ball is contacted on the serve. The remaining five players assume fairly normal positions, with the three forwards as the front line of the W and the two backs as the back line. Refer to Diagrams 20.2, 20.3, and 20.4 for the alignments that are used when the setter is in the three back row positions.

The setter moves to the net, taking a position to the right of center front between the right forward and center forward attackers. The setter faces the left side of the court, the strong side. Refer to the diagrams to view what the pattern of movement is for the setter coming from each of the three back row positions. Note that when the setter is the left back, the distance to move is the greatest. When moving to the net from this position, the setter must keep his or her eyes on the receivers as the ball is passed (see Diagram 20.4).

RULE SUMMARY FOR SUCCESSFUL SERVE RECEPTION

All Players

- decide who will receive the ball as soon as possible after contact by the server,
- call for the ball before it crosses the plane of the net,
- open up to the player playing the ball, and
- help call the ball out-of-bounds for other players.

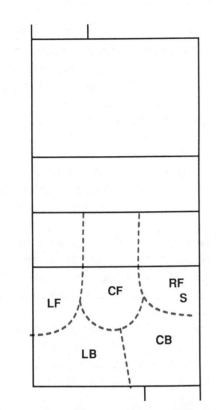

Diagram 20.1 Serve-reception, responsibilities, W-formation, setter is RB, 6–2 offense.

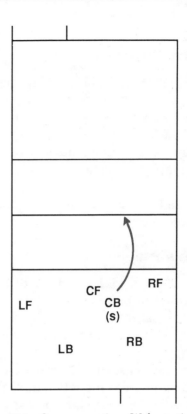

Diagram 20.3 Serve reception, W-formation, setter is CB, 6–2 offense.

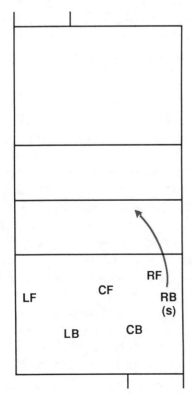

Diagram 20.2 Serve reception, W-formation, setter is RB, 6–2 offense.

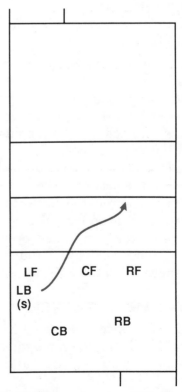

Diagram 20.4 Serve reception, W-formation, setter is LB, 6–2 offense.

Front Row Players

- allow balls that are higher than chest level to be played by back row players,
- do not move back more than one step to play the ball,
- call the ball out on the sideline for the back row player on the same side of the court, and
- are ready to move forward quickly on short serves.

Back Row Players

- allow a ball that is at chest height or higher to go out-of-bounds,
- call the ball out on the sideline for the front row player on the same side of the court,
- are more aggressive from the left back position in receiving when the ball is between the left and right backs,
- call ball out over the end line for each other, and
- always position themselves between the front row players.

Setters

- never receive the serve,
- call short serves,
- call for the pass and extend hand closer to the net high as a target for the passer,
- face the left sideline with the right foot forward in the stride position,
- move to the net as soon as the ball is contacted on the serve,
- hide behind a front row player to prevent the server from serving at them, and
- make sure they keep their eyes on the receiver and the pass throughout the movement from the left back position.

COVERING THE ATTACKER

In the 6–2 offense, covering the attacker can be accomplished with the same three-player semicircle and two players back. However, the alignment of these players is much different from the previous offenses. When covering in the 6–2, the setter is in the middle of the three-player semicircle. The center forward is the player closest to the net.

Refer to Diagrams 20.5, 20.6, and 20.7 for the alignment of players covering the attacker in all three attacking positions when the setter is the right back. When the setter is in the left back and center back positions for serve reception—after penetrating to the net, setting, and moving to cover the attacker—the setter returns to the right back position, remaining there until the next serve. The setter specializes as a right back because it is easiest to move to the net from this position. It is also an area least likely to be attacked by the opponents, because it is the power alley for their weak side. If the setter does not have to dig the ball defensively, the setter is available to direct the attack.

The center forward covers in a position close to the net because it is assumed that this player is always moving to the net for a quick set on every serve reception. If the center forward does not go to the net for a quick attack, the setter finds it difficult to move to a covering position without running into that player.

FREE BALL

In free ball movement in the 6–2, all three attackers move off the net to the attack line, and the setter quickly penetrates to the net from the right back position. The center back must adjust positioning to the right back point of the W. It is extremely important that the setter communicate the free ball call to all teammates, but particularly to the center back. If the center back is unaware that a free ball has been called and does not adjust positioning, the right back area of the court is open and extremely vulnerable. When passing a free ball to the setter, the receivers should use an overhead pass and turn their shoulders in the direction of the pass (see Figure 20.8).

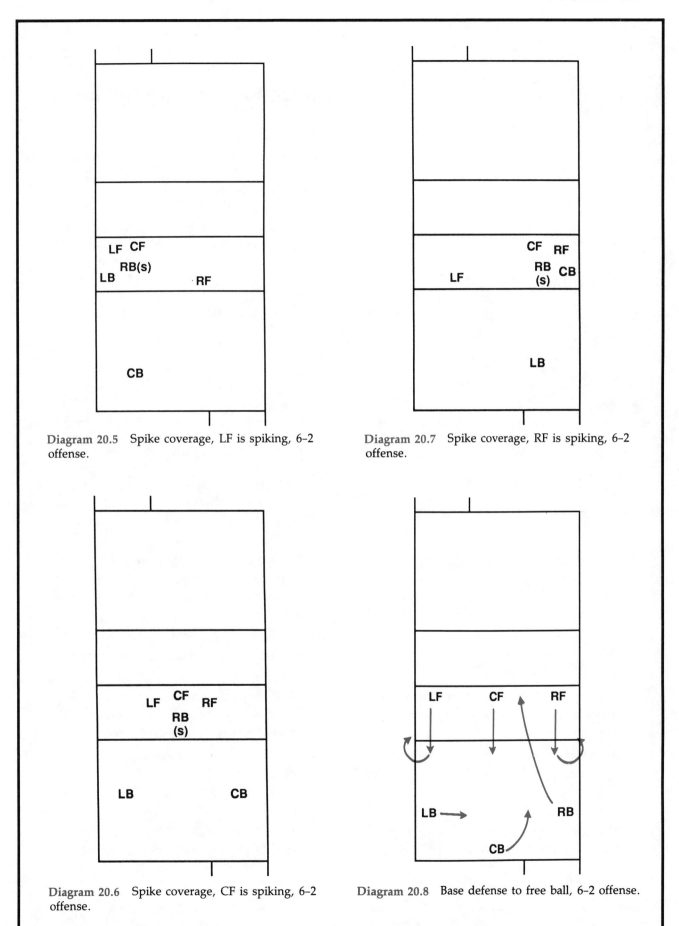

Diagram 20.5   Spike coverage, LF is spiking, 6-2 offense.

Diagram 20.7   Spike coverage, RF is spiking, 6-2 offense.

Diagram 20.6   Spike coverage, CF is spiking, 6-2 offense.

Diagram 20.8   Base defense to free ball, 6-2 offense.

Detecting 6–2 Offense Errors

Most of the errors occurring in serve reception, coverage of the attacker, and free ball formations are due to players either leaving a position prematurely or not adjusting position soon enough. The three most common problem areas are (a) the front line players not moving off the net quick enough on a free ball, (b) the setter penetrating to the net too soon when anticipating a free ball, and (c) the center back not adjusting to the right back area when the setter penetrates to the net.

ERROR

CORRECTION

ERROR	CORRECTION
1. A pass or dig reaches the net before the setter.	1. The setter must move to the net on serve reception as soon as the serve is contacted and must move to the net from a defensive position as soon as it is evident that the attack will not be to the right back area.
2. The attack lands in the right back position with no one to receive it.	2. The setter must realize that the primary responsibility is defense and that the secondary responsibility is to direct the attack.
3. The setter and the center forward collide when trying to cover an attacker.	3. The center forward must charge to the net for a quick attack on each offensive series.
4. A free ball falls between the front row players and the back row players.	4. All three forwards must move quickly to the attack line, set themselves, and be prepared to play a free ball.
5. A free ball over the net lands in the right back position with no one to play it.	5. The setter must communicate the free ball call to all teammates. The center back must adjust when the setter penetrates to the net.
6. The serve falls to the ground between the two back row players in the W.	6. The left back player should be the aggressive player on serve receive when the serve is between the two back players.

6–2 Offense Drills

1. Serve Reception and Attack Drill

A team of six lines up on one side of the court, with a server on the opposite side of the court. The server serves underhand to the receiving team. Using a W-formation with the setter in the right back position, the team receives the serve, executes an attack with any of the three front row attackers, and covers the attacker. The ball must land within the boundaries of the opposite court for the attack to be considered successful.

The team receives 5 good serves, then rotates one position. Drill continues until the players have rotated around to their original starting positions.

Success Goal = 24 out of 30 successful receptions of serve to a completed attack

Your Score = (#) _____ successful attacks

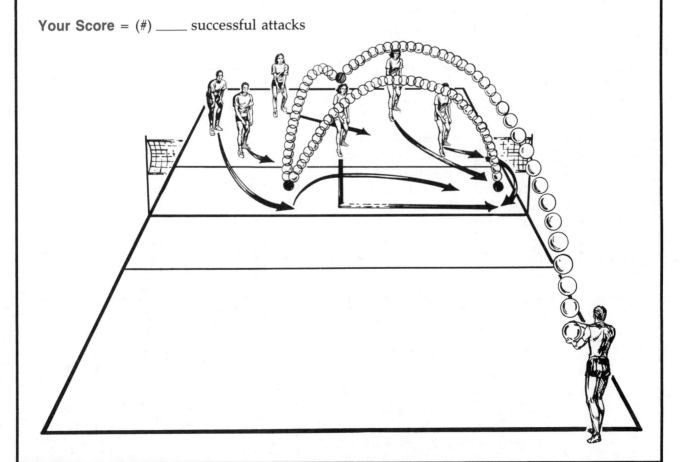

2. Free Ball and Attack Drill

Three attackers, a setter, and a passer set up on one side of the net, and a tosser stands on the opposite side. The three attackers begin in the three front row positions in the base defensive formation. The setter begins in the right back of the court. The passer begins in the left back position.

The tosser yells ''free'' and tosses the ball to the passer. The passer passes to the setter, who has penetrated to the net. At the free ball call, the attackers drop back to the attack line and prepare to hit. The setter sets to one of the three attackers, who makes a successful attack. All players should cover as appropriate. The team receives 15 free balls.

Success Goal = 12 completed attacks in 15 attempts

Your Score = (#) _____ completed attacks

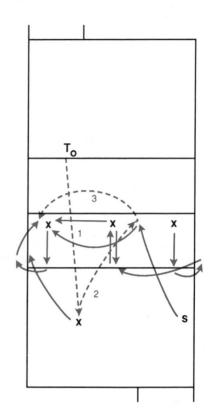

3. Setter Penetration and Right Back Covering Drill

A middle and an outside attacker, a setter, and a center back player set up on one side of the net. A tosser stands on the opposite side of the net.

The tosser yells ''free'' and tosses the ball to the right back corner of the opposite court. At the ''free'' signal, the setter penetrates to the net, and the center back must quickly move to cover the right back area of the court. The center back passes to the setter, who sets to the middle or outside hitters to complete the succesful attack. The team receives 15 free balls.

Success Goal = a. the center back must pass 12 out of 15 free balls to the setter
b. the group must complete 10 out of 12 attacks

Your Score = a. (#) _____ free balls passed to the setter
b. (#) _____ completed attacks

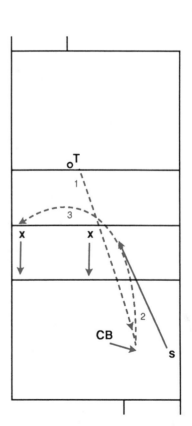

4. Set, Cover, and Recover Drill

Have three setters in the right back position, a passer in the left back position, and three hitters in the left front position on one side of the court.

A tosser on the opposite side of the court tosses the ball over the net to the passer. The passer passes the ball to a setter who has penetrated to the setter's position at the net. The setter sets the ball high outside to the attacker. The setter must follow the set by moving to the coverage position, arriving there before the attacker contacts the ball. As always, the ball must land within the boundaries of the other side on the attack.

After the ball is attacked, the setter quickly returns to the end of the setting line in the right back position, and the attacker goes to the end of the attack line. The tosser immediately tosses the next ball to the passer, and the play is repeated with the second setter and second attacker. The team receives 15 tosses.

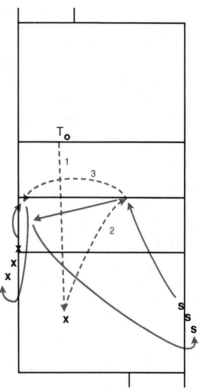

Success Goal = a. 12 good sets and coverages out of 15
  b. 12 successful attacks out of 15

Your Score = a. (#) _____ good sets and coverages
  b. (#) _____ successful attacks

Step 21 2–4 Defense

The 2–4 defense is one of the two most frequently used defenses in volleyball, along with the 2–1–3 defense. The 2–4 defense is more difficult to execute because each player is required to receive two different types of attacks, both the dink and the hard-driven spike. This means that the success of this defense relies heavily upon the ability of the players to read the play of the opponents. The 2–1–3 defense (discussed in Step 18) is often the first one used by a team. Many teams are capable of executing both of these defensive systems and employ the one that proves to be the more successful against a given opponent. It is better to be able to execute one defensive system effectively than to try to use both defensive systems before either is mastered, though.

WHY IS THE 2–4 DEFENSE IMPORTANT?

Generally, as the level of play in volleyball improves, teams are capable of executing more powerful attacks. The 2–1–3 defense becomes less efficient as the attack becomes more powerful. The 2–4 defense allows a team to cover the deep court more completely and, thus, is usually employed against a team with a more powerful attack.

In the 2–4 defense, there is a player positioned in the backcourt behind the block. Having this area protected allows a team to dig balls that are deflected up by the block and go high to the backcourt as well as balls that go through the block. This added protection is needed especially against opponents who utilize a quick middle attack. Often a middle blocker, due to the threat of a middle attack, does not have time to close the block, thus leaving the middle backcourt vulnerable. The extra backcourt player covers this area.

HOW TO EXECUTE THE 2–4 DEFENSE

As in the 2–1–3 defense, there are two basic positions to take when executing the 2–4 defense. The base defensive formation is used when your team is waiting to see what play the opponents will execute. If the opponents are able to execute a spike, your team can counter with a block. If the opponents are unable to attack, your team should drop back into the free ball formation (discussed in steps on offense). It is extremely important that all players on your team move into the same formation. Usually the setter indicates whether your team should block or move to receive a free ball. Sometimes the setter calls a free ball and the opponents, in fact, complete a hard-driven spike. If this happens and all members of your team have assumed the same formation, the court is still sufficiently covered.

BASE

The base defensive formation with the 2–4 defensive system is slightly different from that with the 2–1–3 system. The center back player remains deep in the court and the left back and the right back players remain 5 feet from the sidelines. In the 2–4 defensive alignment, the center back player is positioned on the end line. The starting position for the center back must be deeper than in the 2–1–3, in order to enhance the ability of this player to attain that deep position. The left and right backs adjust their positions about 3–5 feet in from the sideline to cover the center of the court. If this adjustment isn't made, the center of the court is very vulnerable to *setter dumps:* This is when the setter places the second contact over the net rather than directing the attack. Refer to Diagram 21.1 for the correct base defensive position for using the 2–4 defense.

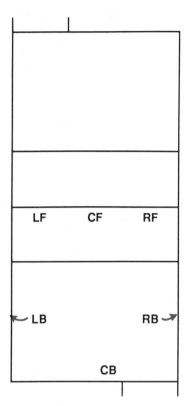

Diagram 21.1 Base defense used for 2–4 defense.

BLOCK

As soon as the location of the opponent's attack is determined, the defending team sets their block and defensive coverage. In the 2–4 defensive system, location of the four backcourt players and their responsibilities are different than in the 2–1–3. Refer to Diagrams 21.2, 21.3, and 21.4 for the correct defensive positioning for attacks from all three opposing forwards.

In the 2–4 defensive alignment, each player has to be prepared to receive any kind of attack. This makes reading the opponent's play extremely important. *Reading* is the ability to intelligently anticipate what the opponents are going to do. The responsibilities of all players are now described for the defense against a right forward attack from the opponents (see Diagrams 21.2 and 21.5). The left back takes a position on the line and is responsible for dinks over the block, spikes down the line,

and off-speed attacks toward the center of the court. The left back should be more aggressive than the right back in defending this center court area. The left back can cover two thirds of the court width, leaving the remaining third to the right back.

The center back remains deep on the end line and is responsible for spikes over the top of the block, spikes deflected by the block, and high, easy balls to either deep corner of the court.

The right back is in the power alley and is responsible for hard-driven spikes that go by the block. The right back lines up with the inside shoulder of the center blocker, with the attacker's hand and ball in view. The right back is also responsible for off-speed attacks to the center of the court and toward the right third of the court.

The right forward moves off the net to the attack line and 10 feet in from the sideline. This player is responsible for dinks to the center of the court close to the net, sharp-angled spikes, and junk off the net.

The responsibilities of all players in aligning to defend against the left forward attacker are basically the same. The players' roles are determined by their positions on the court. The right back takes a position on the line and is responsible for dinks over the block, spikes down-the-line and off-speed attacks toward the center of the court. The left back is in the power alley and is responsible for hard-driven spikes that go by the block and off-speed attacks to the center of the court. The center back remains deep on the end line and is responsible for spikes over the top of the block, spikes deflected by the block, and high, easy balls to either deep corner of the court. The left forward moves off the net to the attack line and 10 feet in from the sideline. This player is responsible for dinks to the center of the court close to the net, sharp-angled spikes, and junk off the net.

In the defense against the center attack, because only one blocker is used, five players cover the backcourt. Both off-blockers move to the attack line and have the responsibilities just described.

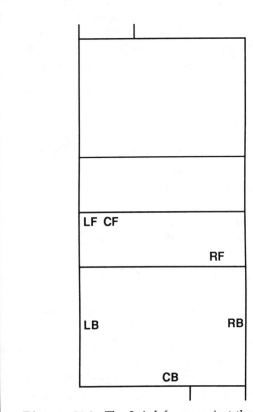

Diagram 21.2 The 2–4 defense against the spike by the opposing RF.

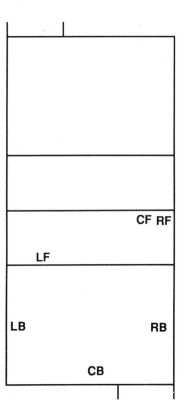

Diagram 21.4 The 2–4 defense against the spike by the opposing LF.

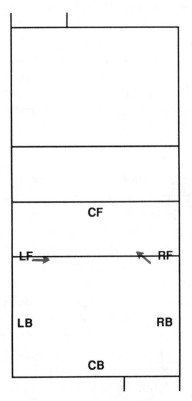

Diagram 21.3 The 2–4 defense against the spike by the opposing CF.

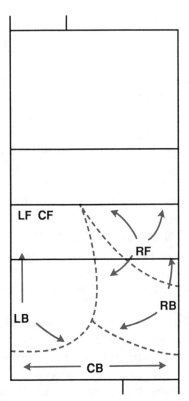

Diagram 21.5 The 2–4 defense against the spike by the opposing RF, showing player responsibilities for each position.

RULE SUMMARY FOR SUCCESSFUL BLOCK DEFENSE

All Players

- should anticipate play of opponents by attempting to read what the opponents will do and
- move to the defensive position, set, and are ready to react before the ball is contacted by the attacker.

Front Row Players

- should have hands at shoulder level or higher in starting position,
- should move along the net left and right but never away from the net and back to the net,
- have no arm swing,
- put hands across net on the block, and
- when playing the off-blocker, move to the attack line ready to play defense.

Backcourt Players

- keep low body posture with weight forward on the toes and
- move through the ball toward the target.

Off-Blocker

- plays dinks to the center of the court,
- plays junk off the net, and
- plays hard-driven spikes at the sharp angle to the sideline.

Center Back

- must stay deep in the court on or behind the end line,
- is responsible for any ball that hits the block and rebounds deep into the court,
- plays any high balls to the corners of the court behind the two line players, and
- must react by moving forward to cover the middle of the court if the blocker does not close the block.

Defensive Player on the Line

- must play any spike down-the-line, and
- must be ready to move forward and dig any dink over the block directed down the line.

Power Alley Player

- aligns so that the inside shoulder of the middle blocker, the ball, and the attacker's hand are all in view, and
- receives spikes or off-speeds into the power alley.

Detecting 2–4 Defense Errors

The most common errors a team makes when executing the 2–4 defense are associated with the players' lack of ability in determining who should play the ball. You should not decide in advance who should or should not play the ball; you should simply react to the play as it develops. Players are positioned on the court in such a way that when two of you move to the ball at the same time, one should always be in front of the other, and you should cross rather than collide. Concern about colliding with a teammate may cause you to stop rather than play through the ball.

ERROR   **CORRECTION**

1. The center back player attempts to dig an off-speed attack to the middle of the court.

2. A ball dug by the setter does not get set.

3. The dink over the block falls to the court without being dug.

4. The line player behind the block ducks when a spike down the line is chest high or higher.

5. A deep dink falls to either back corner of the court.

6. A spiked ball goes through the block and hits the floor.

1. The center back player must remain deep on the end line; the left back or right back is responsible for off-speed attacks to this area.

2. The setter, after digging the attack, is not eligible to make the second contact or set; in this situation the player in the right forward position assumes the setting role.

3. The player on the sideline on the same side of the block is responsible for spikes down-the-line and dinks over the block.

4. The line player must play this spike, even if just by raising the arms and blocking it.

5. The center back is responsible for covering deep, easy balls to both corners of the court.

6. If the middle blocker doesn't close the block, the center back must move forward in anticipation of a spike to the center of the court.

2–4 Defense Drills

1. Six-Player Defensive Drill

A team of six sets up on one side of the court in base defensive position. A tosser, setter, and three attackers set up on the opposite side.

The tosser overhand tosses the ball to the setter, who sets any of the attackers. The setter should disguise which attacker will be set, so that the defense must react to the attack as though in a game. The attacker spikes over the net.

The defending team must either block the spike, or receive it and attempt to execute a counterattack. If the attacking players are unable to spike, the defending team should move to a free ball position to receive the third hit over. When the defending team successfully makes the transition and executes the attack, they must cover the attacker.

The defending team should receive 5 attacks, then rotate one position. Continue until all players are back in their original positions.

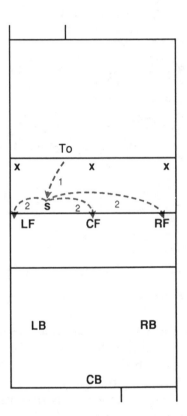

Success Goal = 20 successful blocks or digs and counterattacks out of 30 spikes

Your Score = (#) _____ blocks or digs and counterattacks

2. Digging the Power Attack Drill

A team of six sets up on one side of the court. On the other side, a spiker in the left front position stands on a box with a feeder alongside.

The spiker self-tosses the ball high enough to allow the middle blocker to join the outside blocker, then attacks cross-court. The team attempts to dig the spike and complete an attack in transition. The ball must land inbounds on the attack.

As usual, the drill is run with 5 spikes, followed by the team rotating one position.

Success Goal = a. 20 good digs out of 30 spikes
b. 15 out of 30 completed attacks

Your Score = a. (#) _____ good digs
b. (#) _____ completed attacks

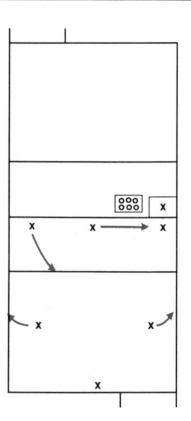

3. Setter Digs and Right Forward Sets Drill

This uses the same formation as the previous drill. Here, though, the left forward on the box spikes down-the-line. This forces the right back (setter) to dig the ball, which means that another player must set. It is preferable that the right forward sets in this situation.

This drill is run with 5 spikes before the team rotates one position.

Success Goal = a. 20 out of 30 successful digs
b. 15 out of 30 completed attacks

Your Score = a. (#) _____ digs
b. (#) _____ attacks

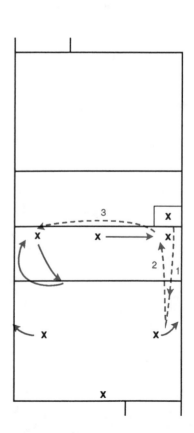

4. Covering Cross-Court Dinks Drill

This drill uses the same formation as the previous two drills. Now, though, the left forward on the box dinks the ball toward the center of the court close to the net. The left forward of the opposing team should dig this dink.

This drill runs with 5 dinks followed by the team rotating.

Success Goal = a. 20 out of 30 successful digs
b. 15 out of 30 completed attacks

Your Score = a. (#) _____ digs
b. (#) _____ attacks

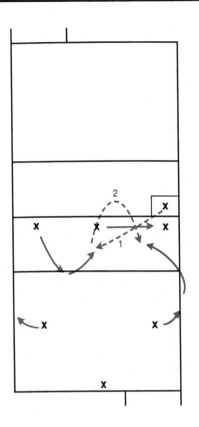

5. Digging Deep Dinks to the Right Back Corner Drill

This drill uses the same formation as the three previous drills. However, the left forward dinks or passes the ball high to the right back corner of the opposing court. The center back defensive player should dig this ball as the setter penetrates to the net.

This drill is run with 5 dinks or passes; then the team rotates.

Success Goal = a. 20 out of 30 successful digs
b. 15 out of 30 completed attacks

Your Score = a. (#) _____ digs
b. (#) _____ attacks

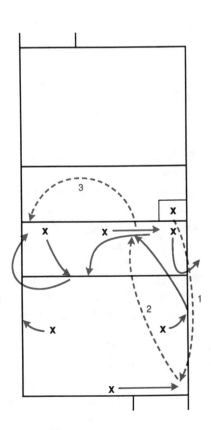

Step 22 5–1 Offense

The 5–1 offense is the offensive system that is used most frequently at the international level of play. The 5–1 offense uses only one setter. This means that during three rotations, the setter is in the front row; during the other three rotations, the setter penetrates to the net from the back row. The other five players are attackers, with the player opposite the setter being called the *off-side attacker*.

It is extremely beneficial, if your team specializes, to use a left-hander as the off-side attacker because this player would be hitting from the right front position, which is a left-hander's strong side. The setter can become extremely deceptive and effective in attacking the second hit and sending it to the opponents as either a hard-driven attack, a dink, or an off-speed attack. This allows the team to attack from all three positions. Furthermore, it is advantageous to have a left-handed setter because it is easier for such a setter to attack on-hand.

WHY IS THE 5–1 OFFENSE IMPORTANT?

The 5–1 offense is the best offense for any team that has only one setter. Many coaches feel that this offense is the best and most efficient because every attacker hits the sets of only one setter. Attackers do not have to worry about a second setter who has different timing in the sets; if they hit off only one setter, they become very accustomed to that player and do not need to adjust each time the second setter takes over the setting role.

The setter can also attack when in the front row; therefore, more options are available on the second contact. The setter must also be an extremely good blocker. Teams with a short setter are at a disadvantage when the setter is in the front row. Shorter players can be very effective spikers if the ball is set off the net, but is very difficult for them to block unless they are excellent jumpers.

When using the 5–1 offense, a team can also employ a variety of serve reception patterns that attempt to hide the front row or back row status of the setter. Some opposing teams forget to watch for this and are surprised when the setter attacks the ball on the second contact as a front row player, because they are thinking that the setter is in the back row. This option can often be extremely effective. The setter in a 5–1 offense should make good use of this play.

HOW TO EXECUTE THE 5–1 OFFENSE

Once a team has mastered the International 4–2 and 6–2 offensive systems, learning the 5–1 is fairly simple. The 5–1 combines the actions of these two other offenses, actually using each one for half of the total rotations. During three rotations, the setter is a back row player, and formations are the same as in the 6–2. During the other three rotations, the setter is a front row player, and the formations are the same as the International 4–2.

SERVE RECEPTION

When the setter is in the back row, the W-formation serve reception pattern is exactly the same as in the 6–2 offense. The setter hides behind a front row player and moves to the net as soon as the ball is contacted on the serve, remembering to keep the eyes on the receivers at all times. The setter must be in a set position when receiving the pass. The setter then directs the offense and follows the set to cover the attack. After covering, the setter returns to the right back position on the court and prepares for defending against an attack by the opponent.

When the setter is a front row player, the serve reception is the same as that used in the International 4–2 offensive system. The setter can take a position at the net or in such a manner that it appears as if the setter is penetrating from a back row position to the net. Diagrams 22.1, 22.2, and 22.3 show the second method of lining up when the setter is a front row player and the team attempts to disguise that fact.

When the setter attempts to disguise his or her location, the setter must make sure that overlapping of the player next to that position does not occur. Once the ball is contacted on the serve, the setter assumes the right forward position and remains there until the next serve.

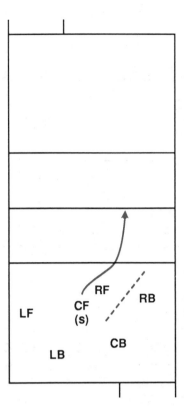

Diagram 22.2 Serve reception, setter is CF, using 5–1 offense.

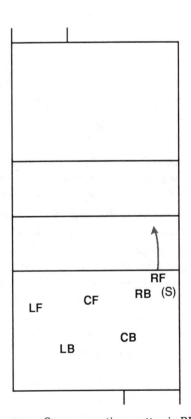

Diagram 22.1 Serve reception, setter is RF, using 5–1 offense.

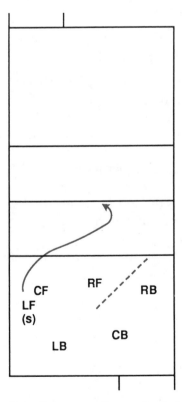

Diagram 22.3 Serve reception, setter is LF, using 5–1 offense.

RULE SUMMARY FOR SUCCESSFUL SERVE RECEPTION

All Players

- decide who will receive the ball as soon as possible after contact by the server,
- call for the ball before it crosses the plane of the net,
- open up to the player playing the ball, and
- help call the ball out-of-bounds for other players.

Front Row Players

- allow balls that are higher than chest level to be played by back row players,
- do not move back more than one step to play the ball,
- call the ball out on the sideline for the back row player on the same side of the court, and
- are ready to move forward quickly on short serves.

Back Row Players

- allow a ball that is at chest height or higher to go out-of-bounds,
- call the ball out on the sideline for the front row player on the same side of the court,
- are more aggressive from the left back position in receiving when the ball is between the left and right backs,
- call ball out over the end line for the other back, and
- always position themselves between the front row players.

Setters

- never receive the serve,
- call short serves,
- call for the pass and extend hand closer to the net high as a target for the passer, and
- face the left sideline with the right foot forward in the stride position.

Setters (Back Row)

- move to the net as soon as the ball is contacted on the serve,
- hide behind a front row player to prevent server from serving at them, and
- keep eyes on the receiver and the pass when moving from the left back position.

COVERING THE ATTACKER

In the 5–1 offensive system, covering the attacker is the same as it is for the 6–2 offense when the setter is in the back row, and identical to the International 4–2 offense when the setter is in the front row (refer to Steps 19 and 20). The 3–2 coverage is used, with the three-person semicircle around the attacker and two players filling the spaces in the back court.

FREE BALL

As for serve reception and covering the attacker, the pattern continues: The free ball formation for the 5–1 offense is identical to the formation used in the 6–2 offense when the setter is in the back row, and identical to the International 4–2 when the setter is in the front row (refer to Steps 19 and 20). When the setter is a front row player, the right back player must always remember to move toward the attack line as if playing a forward position. The right back position seems to be the one that is most difficult to learn.

Detecting 5–1 Offense Errors

Because the 5–1 offense is a combination of the International 4–2 and the 6–2, the errors associated with these two systems are the same as the errors for the 5–1. During the three rotations when the setter is a front row player, the errors would be the same as the errors found in the International 4–2. When the setter is penetrating from the back row for the other three rotations, the errors would be the same as found in the 6–2.

ERROR 🚫 **CORRECTION**

Setter in Front Row

1. The setter receives the serve.

1. Setter should hide at the net and not receive the serve under any circumstances.

2. A free ball falls between a front row player and a back row player.

2. The two forwards must move off the net to the attack line as quickly as possible and assume a ready position prior to the opponent making contact with the ball that is being sent over the net.

3. The ball rebounds off the opponent's block and falls to the floor on the attacker's side.

3. Three players must assume a coverage position around the attacker.

4. A player in the W-formation gets hit on the back by a passed ball.

4. All players must open up to the receiver by turning and facing that player.

5. The serve falls to the court between two players.

5. Receivers must call for the serve prior to the ball's crossing the net.

6. The ball rebounds off the block and falls to the court between the coverage and the sideline.

6. The player covering closest to the line should have the outside foot on the sideline and should not play any ball that rebounds off the block beyond the sideline side of the body.

7. The attacker prevents the coverage from playing the ball.

7. The attacker should not play a ball that rebounds off the block, unless it stays between the attacker and the net.

ERROR   **CORRECTION**

8. A free ball falls to the court in the right forward position.

9. The setter attempts to back set.

8. The setter is the right forward and remains at the net; therefore, the right back must adjust and cover this area of the court.

9. The two eligible attackers are in the center forward and left forward positions; there is no right forward attacker.

Setter in Back Row

1. A pass or dig reaches the net before the setter.

2. The attack lands in the right back position with no one to receive it.

3. The setter and the center forward collide when trying to cover an attacker.

4. A free ball falls between the front row players and the back row players.

5. A third ball over the net lands in the right back position with no one to play it.

6. The serve falls to the court between the two back row players in the W.

1. In receiving service, the setter must move to the net as soon as the serve is contacted; defending against an attack, the setter must move to the net from a defensive position as soon as it is evident that the attack will not be to the right back area.

2. The setter must realize that the primary responsibility is defense and that the secondary responsibility is to direct the attack.

3. The center forward must charge to the net for a possible quick attack on each offensive series. If the center forward does not charge to the net, the setter will collide with this player as they both move to cover.

4. All three forwards must move quickly to the attack line, set themselves, and be prepared to play a free ball.

5. The setter must communicate the free ball call to all teammates. The center back must adjust when the setter penetrates to the net.

6. The left back player should be the aggressive player on serve receive when the serve is between the two back players.

5–1 Offense Drills

1. Set, Cover, and Recover Drill

Have three setters stand in the right back position, a passer in the left back position, and three hitters in the left front position on one side of the court. A tosser stands on the opposite side of the court.

The tosser tosses the ball over the net to the passer. The passer passes the ball to a setter, who has penetrated to the setter's position at the net. The setter sets the ball high and outside to the attacker. The setter must follow the set to the coverage position, arriving there before the attacker contacts the ball. The attack must be inbounds.

After the ball is attacked, the setter quickly returns to the end of the setting line in the right back position, and the attacker goes to the end of the attack line. The tosser immediately tosses the next ball to the passer, and the play is repeated with the second setter and attacker. The team receives 15 tosses.

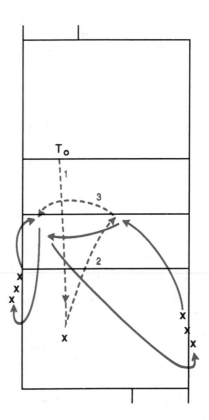

Success Goal = a. setters make 12 good sets out of 15 followed by correct coverage

b. group completes 10 good attacks out of 12 attempts

Your Score = a. (#) _____ sets and coverages

b. (#) _____ complete attacks

2. Free Ball Attack Drill

Three attackers, a setter, and a passer set up
on one side of the net. The three attackers begin in the three front row positions in the base
defensive formation. The setter begins in the
right back of the court. The passer begins in
the left back position.

A tosser on the other side of the net yells
"free" and tosses the volleyball to the passer.
The passer passes to the setter, who has
penetrated to the net. At the free ball call, the
attackers drop back to the attack line and prepare to hit. The setter sets to one of the three
attackers. All players should cover as appropriate. The team receives 15 free balls.

Success Goal = 12 good attacks out of 15 free balls

Your Score = (#) _____ good attacks

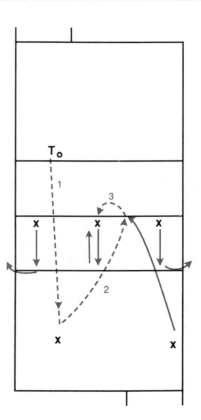

3. Setter Penetration and Right Back Covering Drill

A middle attacker, an outside attacker, a setter,
and a center back player set up on one side
of the net.

A tosser on the opposite side of the net yells
"free" and tosses the ball to the right back
corner of the opposite court. At the "free" signal, the setter penetrates to the net, and the
center back must quickly move to cover the
right back area of the court. The center back
passes to the setter, who sets to the middle
or outside hitter to complete the attack. The
team receives 15 free balls.

Success Goal = a. center back makes 12 good
passes out of 15 to the setter
b. group completes 10 out of
12 attacks

Your Score = a. (#) _____ passes
b. (#) _____ completed attacks

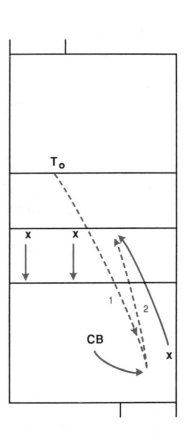

4. Free Ball Drill

A team of six lines up on one side of the court. The three forwards are at the net in blocking position. The center back is in the center of the court, and the left and right backs are on their respective sidelines 20 feet from the net.

A tosser on the opposite side of the net yells ''free,'' delays for a couple of seconds, then tosses the ball over the net high and easy. The team of six quickly moves into the W-formation, receives the ball, sets an attack, and covers the attacker.

The team receives 5 balls, then rotates one position. Continue this drill until the players have rotated around to their original starting positions.

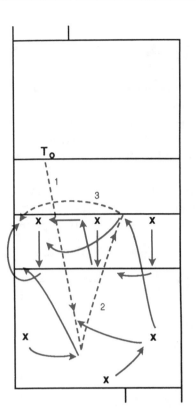

Success Goal = 24 out of 30 successful attacks with the proper coverage

Your Score = (#) _____ successful attacks with the proper coverage

5. Cover and Dig Drill

A team of six sets up on one side of the court in the W-formation, with the setter in the center forward position. On the opposite side of the net, two blockers stand on a box on the right side of the court.

A tosser on the same court as the blockers yells ''free'' and throws a high ball over the net. The team receives the free ball, sets an attack to their left forward, and covers. The blockers block the ball, and the coverage attempts to dig successfully, which means being able to set up for a second attack.

The team receives 5 tosses, then rotates one position. This drill continues until the players have returned to their original positions.

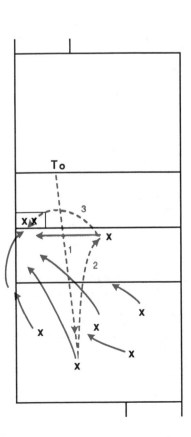

Success Goal = 18 out of 30 successful digs off the opposing blocks

Your Score = (#) _____ digs

6. *Serve and Free Ball Drill*

A team of six starts in the W-formation. A tosser and a server are on the opposite side of the net, each with a ball.

The server serves. The receiving team passes the serve, sets their attack, and covers.

The team immediately assumes starting positions as in Drill 4. The tosser calls "free" and tosses the ball high over the net. The receiving team passes the free ball, sets an attack, and covers.

Play continues with another serve, followed by another free ball. The team receives 5 good serves alternating with 5 free balls, then rotates one position. The drill continues until all players rotate around to their starting positions.

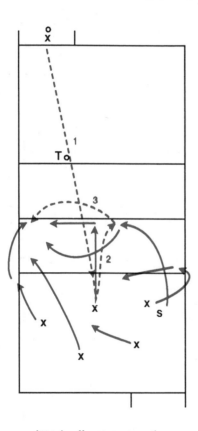

Attack off serve reception

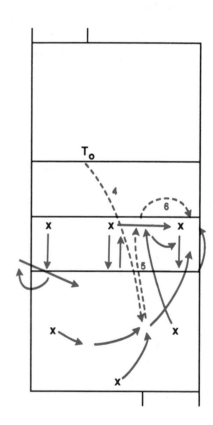

Attack off free ball

Success Goal = a. 24 out of 30 successful attacks off serves with the correct coverage
b. 24 out of 30 successful attacks off free balls with the correct coverage

Your Score = a. (#) _____ attacks off serves
b. (#) _____ attacks off free balls

7. *Setter Attacks Second Ball Drill*

On one side of the court stand a passer in the left back position and a setter in the right front position. A tosser and a blocker (left front) are on the opposite court.

The tosser tosses the ball over the net to the passer. The passer passes the ball to the setter, who attacks the ball using either an off-speed spike, a hard-driven spike, or a dink. Off-speed hits should be directed past the blocker toward the center of the opponent's court, dinks toward the center of the court or to the sideline behind the left front blocker. Setter attacks 15 passes.

Success Goal = 10 out of 15 successful attacks

Your Score = (#) _____ attacks

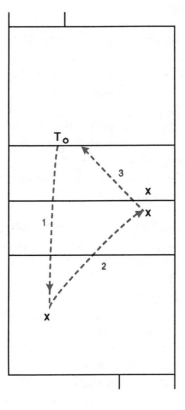

Step 23   Game Situation

Now that you have mastered all the basic skills and several options for offensive and defensive strategies, you are ready to play a legal game against an opponent. Of course, your team needs to make several decisions before the competition begins.

1. What offensive system are you going to use?
2. What defensive system will you try?
3. Who will be your setters?
4. Who are your strongest attackers, servers, and defensive players?
5. What are the strengths of your opponents?
6. Who will be your court leader to call and direct the play?

Your choice of offense depends on the quality and type of players that make up your team. If you have only four strong spikers, then a 4-2 offense is the best choice. If you have six, then a 6-2 offense would offer more options. If you wish to use a 6-2, your setters must be quick and mobile.

Defensively, you need tall, good blockers to use a 2-1-3. If you have a weak defensive player or slow setter, the 2-1-3 is an excellent choice because the weak player or setter can be placed behind the block, where he or she will not have to receive a spiked ball.

The setters must have exceptional setting ability and must be able to assume leadership roles. A setter is often selected as the player who will call the court movements for the team.

It is advantageous to the coach submitting the lineup to place all of the players in strategic starting positions. You would like to have your best server serving first. You also want your best attacker in the left forward or left back position because someone starting there would be a forward for the longest amount of time. The best defensive player should begin in either the right forward or right back position, and your best passers should always be in the back row. The strongest setter should be the first one to assume the setting role.

You must select a court leader. This individual will be the person who directs the play on the court (refer to ''Signaling for Success'' later in this step). The person should be a natural leader and ready to direct the attack and defense in an aggressive manner.

Once decisions have been made on these organizational aspects of play, you are ready to begin the game. The choice of either taking first serve or picking the starting court goes to the team that wins the toss; the other team has the remaining selection.

Once the game is underway, all players have to make decisions constantly about where they are supposed to be and the nature of their responsibilities. Volleyball is a game of constant movement and decision making. With each contact of the ball by your own team or by your opponents, you must anticipate the upcoming result and position yourself strategically.

If you do not do this, weak or open areas will exist on your court, and you will be vulnerable to the opponent's attack. Your team is only as strong as its weakest player; as soon as an opponent discovers who that player is, they will take advantage of this by playing the ball to that player's court area. Your team must try to play all of its players in positions that enhance the strength of the entire team.

SPECIALIZATION

Rotation is a characteristic that differentiates volleyball from other sports. All players rotate to a new position on the court each time their team earns a sideout. This means that each player must learn the characteristics of six different positions. This is extremely difficult. It is also very time-consuming in practice sessions because new formations must be practiced in all six rotations.

Specialization of players is a method that helps this problem. Players have to remain on the court in their correct rotational positions only until the ball is served. Then they are allowed to move to any position either on or off the court, with the exception that back row players cannot spike or block from in front of the attack line. As soon as the ball is contacted on the serve, all players may switch to their playing positions. This is usually done by the defensive team as soon as the ball is contacted on the serve, and by the offensive team either after the pass or after the ball is returned over the net.

When players specialize, they each play only one position on the court while they are in the front row and only one position when they are in the back row. Some teams like to keep the players on the same side of the court in both the front and back rows; players might play only on the left side, only in the middle, or only on the right side. Each one of these positions has certain characteristics that are important. The setter usually plays on the right side, and must be a leader, an excellent blocker, quick, and perceptive. The left side player must be a strong, dependable hitter and a strong digger. The middle player must be capable of excellent lateral movement, strong blocking, and hitting a quick, low set.

Using specialization allows a coach to place players where their strengths are of greatest help to their team. Specialization makes it easier for players to learn court positioning because they have to learn only two positions instead of six. It also enhances efficient use of practice time because each new formation has to be practiced in only two rotations. Most highly skilled teams use specialization.

SIGNALING FOR SUCCESS

Communication among players is essential to success on the volleyball court. It is important to realize that actions speak louder than words, and an action by a player signals an intent to a teammate. If that player does not complete the action, then the teammate cannot be expected to, either. A good example of this is during serve reception. If a front line

player moves as if to receive a ball and the back line player behind observes this, the back line player assumes the forward will receive the ball even if the front line player does not call "mine"; the back player stops moving toward the ball. This usually results in no reception, which immediately gives a point to the opponents.

On the other hand, nonverbal signals can often be used to your team's advantage. Opening up to the ball is an example of this. If a front row player opens up to the backcourt, that movement indicates a plan not to receive the ball.

Every team must have a series of verbal signals that the players use to communicate their intentions. The following verbal signals will help your team to play as a unit. All players must know the signals and follow them:

1. Call "mine," "ball," or "I have it" when you are going to play a ball. Team members should call for every ball, but it is of utmost importance to call for the reception of the first ball over the net, especially.
2. Call "out" to indicate that the ball is outside the court boundaries.
3. Call "deep" or "short" to indicate whether the ball should be received by a front line player or a back line player.
4. Call "dink" or "tip" when the opponents indicate they will use that type of attack.
5. Call "over" when the next hit must go over the net to the opponents.
6. Call "touch" when, as a blocker, you contact the opponent's spike, but it remains on your side to be played by your backcourt defense.

In addition to the above signals that are used by all team members, the setter will use the following signals that are specific to that position. These signals are essential in helping all team members execute the same formation at the appropriate time. If the setter does not signal the play, teammates may choose to move into different positions, at the same time causing areas of the court to be insufficiently covered.

1. Call "setter" when you receive the first ball over the net and, thus, cannot make the second contact or set. This tells your teammates someone else must set, the right forward if possible.
2. Call "help" when you cannot make the second contact or set. The closest teammate should make the second contact.
3. Call "free" when it becomes evident that the opponents will not complete their attack.
4. Call "block" when you need to defend against the opponent's attack.
5. Call "cover" after each set to remind your teammates to cover the upcoming attack.

The setter should also signal either verbally or with a hand signal what attack will be used. There are many systems of attack and no standard numbering system in the United States. The net can be divided into 7, 8, or 9 areas. The type of set is often described with two numbers. The first number refers to the area or zone of the net where the set will be placed, the second number to the height of the set. A team can establish its own play-calling system. In this book, we have concentrated on high sets so the setter would need to communicate only which attacker is about to be set.

The attacker(s) who will not be attacking must be sure not to move to coverage before the set is actually made, because sometimes the setter needs to change the direction of the set, due to a poor pass. Every attacker must be ready to receive a set until the ball is actually set; then they can move to the appropriate coverage.

MODIFIED GAMES

Often times it is to a team's advantage to modify the game situation in order to emphasize practice and improvement in specific aspects of strategy. Several examples of this are used in the drills presented in the offensive and defensive steps. For instance, Drill 3: Setter Penetration and Right Back Covering in Step 20 is set up to practice the idea of player movement and court coverage during a free ball situation. In this drill only the key players in the movement are used. This same game aspect can be practiced by modifying a typical game situation utilizing two teams of six players. This can be accomplished as follows:

- Two teams line up on either side of the net. A tosser will be positioned outside the boundaries of the court on one side of the net with a generous supply of volleyballs. Both teams will begin in base defensive formation with the setter in the right back position. The tosser will yell "free," tossing the ball over the net to the right back corner of the opposite side. The team receiving the toss quickly moves into the free ball formation with the setter moving to the net and the center back moving to cover the right back area of the court. Game play will continue until the ball becomes dead. Another toss is initiated to the same team. The tosser makes a given number of tosses to one team, changes sides, and repeats the same number to the opposite team. Score can be kept by awarding one point to the team winning the rally.

By keeping players in the same rotational positions for an extended time period, they have the opportunity to perfect their responsibilities of the rotation. This enhances learning more than a regulation game in which one team rotates with every side out.

- The same procedure can be followed to emphasize two other aspects of team reception of a free ball: (a) the attackers slowly moving off the net and not getting into position soon enough to receive the free ball and (b) the forwards moving directly into the wing out position rather than making their movement straight back and then winging out. To correct situation (a), the tosser would direct the ball to the attackers at the attack line; to correct situation (b), the tosser would direct the ball to either the right or the left forward, but more toward the center of the court than the sideline.

Other suggested game modifications:

- Serving 5 consecutive serves from one side of the net regardless of the result of the rally; then 5 serves by the opposite team. This 5–5 process can continue for each of the six rotations. Score can be kept by awarding 1 point to the team winning the rally.
- To practice defense, a teacher or coach can stand on a box in one of the two outside attack positions spiking the ball at one of the teams. The teacher can either spike the ball to a designated position for a given number of trials or can vary the attack, direction, and type with each trial. After every 5 attacks, the team rotates one position. Score can be kept by awarding 1 point to the team winning the rally. Care should be taken by the setter during this drill not to set the position where the box is located.

These examples show how teams can practice in a scrimmage situation while concentrating their efforts on one aspect of game strategy. Other possibilities exist and are limited only by the creativity of the instructor.

Step 24 Game Play Choices

Each time the ball comes to your team from the opponent, you have to make a decision as to the best method of playing the ball in order to complete the transition from defense to offense in the most efficient manner possible. The decision on how to receive the ball depends upon the type of ball that is returned to your team by the opponents. You want to be able to execute the three-hit combination—pass, set, and attack—each time you receive the ball. The first contact is very important because if you control the ball on the pass, you can easily achieve a good attack.

Usually it is a disadvantage to return the ball to the opponents on the first contact. There is one time, however, when returning the ball on the first contact is extremely effective. If the opponents return the ball to you high, easy, and close to the net (a free ball), your team should immediately spike it back. This play is a high-percentage play and usually results in a point or a side out for your team. If your team returns that type of ball to the opponents, you can expect the same response. Returning the first contact to the opponents in an easy manner is ill-advised unless you place the ball deep to either back corner of the court.

The second contact can be returned to the opponents effectively as a spike if the setter is a front row player or if an attacker has good position on the ball and can spike the pass. It is important that the attacker communicates this intent to the setter so that a collision between the two does not result. The setter can also effectively send the second contact over the net by dinking it. This can be done whether the setter is a front row or a back row player. The back row setter must be careful not to cross the plane of the top of the net in playing the ball over, because this is an illegal play.

Completing the three-hit combination is the most effective offense and is used the majority

of the time. A smart setter can constantly keep the opponents guessing by varying the attack and occasionally sending the second contact over the net, though. If this play is used too often, however, it becomes ineffective.

Following is a list of options available on each of the three contacts, with the choices listed in order of preference.

OFFENSIVE SKILL OPTIONS

First Contact—Receiving

Serve

1. Forearm pass
2. Dig with one arm
3. Overhead pass (often illegal)

Free Ball

1. Spike
2. Overhead pass
3. Forearm pass

Spike

1. Dig with two arms
2. Dig with one arm
3. Dig and roll, or dig and sprawl

Dink

1. Forearm pass
2. Dig with two arms
3. Dig with one arm
4. Dig and roll, or dig and sprawl

Second Contact—Receiving

Pass

1. Set to a spiker
2. Spike over the net
3. Dink over the net
4. Forearm pass to a spiker

Third Contact—Receiving

Set

1. Spike over the net
2. Dink over the net
3. Off-speed spike over the net
4. Spike hit with no jump and good placement
5. Overhead pass to deep corners
6. Forearm pass over the net (not recommended)

DEFENSIVE SKILL RESPONSES

Receiving a Spike

Front Row

1. Three- or two-person block
2. One-person block
3. No block
4. Free ball position

Back Row

1. Dig the ball and keep it on your own side
2. Dig the ball and send it over the net and in-bounds

Your team can enhance its ability to make the correct game choices by anticipating the actions of your opponents. This ability is referred to as *reading* the opponent's play. If you read the opponents well, you will seldom be caught off guard. Your teammates need to communicate constantly about any clues that you read from your opponent's play. Your team must be in position by the time the ball is contacted on the third hit by the opponent. If not in a set position at that time, you may be too late.

SUMMARY

You have now completed the 24 steps in learning the game of volleyball. Each step in this process, although a separate entity, has helped you increase your skill and knowledge of the game as a whole.

At this stage, you have mastered the skills and strategies of volleyball at a level that permits you to successfully participate in a competitive situation. It is our hope that this knowledge will allow you to enjoy playing the game and stimulate your desire to continue to improve through additional practice and playing experience.

Rating Your Game Success

The best place to test your new skills is within a game. Rating can be done either by yourself or by a teacher, coach, or trained partner. Included below are two recommended means of self-evaluation and teacher evaluation.

SELF-EVALUATION

Reflect back on three game performances to rate yourself. Using the checklist below, choose the appropriate response for each question that best describes your performance.

1. I typically serve
   a. to the most strategic place on the opponent's court.
   b. to the seam between two players.
   c. to the opponent's weakest player.
   d. into the opponent's court.
2. I score _____% on a written test covering the basic rules.
   a. 90
   b. 80
   c. 70
   d. 60
3. I score _____% on a written test covering concepts, techniques, and strategies.
   a. 90
   b. 80
   c. 70
   d. 60
4. When receiving serve, I typically pass the ball
   a. to the target area.
   b. to the center of the court—settable, but not perfect.
   c. so that it is not settable, causing my team to send the opponent a free ball.
   d. so poorly, the opponent is awarded an ace.
5. I compliment other players' good hits and efforts
   a. at all times.
   b. most of the time.
   c. seldom.
   d. not at all.

6. I spike
   a. to open areas of the opponent's court.
   b. between two opponents.
   c. right at the opponent's block or right at the opponent's back row defensive players.
   d. out-of-bounds or into the net.
7. When I am going to play the ball, I call for it
   a. always.
   b. most of the time.
   c. seldom.
   d. never.
8. If a teammate calls for the ball, I let that person play it
   a. always.
   b. most of the time.
   c. seldom.
   d. never.
9. When playing the second contact, I
   a. set a spiker.
   b. forearm pass to the spiker.
   c. send the ball over the net.
   d. make an error.
10. When receiving a free ball, I
    a. spike it if possible.
    b. pass it with an overhead pass to the setter.
    c. pass it with a forearm pass to the setter.
    d. send it back over the net.
11. Any time I dig a spike, I
    a. stay on my feet and use two hands.
    b. stay on my feet and use one hand.
    c. dive or roll only when it is needed.
    d. roll or dive whether I need to or not.
12. When my team is on defense, I
    a. read the opponent's play and set myself in the best defensive position.
    b. set my position at the same spot every time.
    c. get into my position late and have difficulty making the play.
    d. watch the opponent's play and never get into position.

13. When a teammate is receiving serve, I
    a. open up to the ball and then get ready for the next play.
    b. watch the ball over my shoulder and then get ready for the next play.
    c. don't watch the ball, but immediately get ready for the next play.
    d. don't watch the ball and never get ready for the next play.
14. When I am a forward and my team is receiving a free ball, I
    a. move straight back to the attack line, play the ball, and/or wing out to the side to get ready to hit.
    b. move straight back to the sideline, play the ball, and/or remain in that position.
    c. move off the court to be ready for the attack, not being concerned about playing the ball.
    d. remain at the net, turn, and watch my teammates play the ball.
15. When a teammate is spiking, I
    a. quickly move to cover the spike and set myself in a low position before the ball is spiked, ready to play the ball off the block.
    b. quickly move to cover the spike and set myself in a medium or high position before the ball is spiked, ready to play the ball off the block.
    c. move to cover the spike, but I am not set before the ball is spiked.
    d. stand in my initial position and applaud when my teammate makes a good spike.
16. When serving, I make
    a. 9 successful serves out of 10 attempts.
    b. 7 successful serves out of 10 attempts.
    c. 6 successful serves out of 10 tries.
    d. 5 or less successful serves out of 10 efforts.

17. When passing a free ball, I make (#) _____ perfect passes to the target area out of 10 attempts.
    a. 9
    b. 8
    c. 7
    d. 6 or less
18. When receiving serve, I pass (#) _____ to the target area out of 10 receptions.
    a. 8
    b. 7
    c. 6
    d. 5 or less
19. When blocking an opponent's spike, I am successful (#) _____ times out of 10.
    a. 4
    b. 3
    c. 2
    d. 1 or less
20. When spiking, I successfully place the ball into the opponent's court (#) _____ times out of 10 tries.
    a. 8
    b. 7
    c. 5 or 6
    d. 4 or less

Choice a is always the best selection, and choice d is the least preferred. After you have completed the 20 items, calculate your total score by awarding yourself 3 points for every a selected, 2 points for every b, 1 point for every c, and 0 points for each d. Your final score is the total number of points. Your overall rating is then figured by the following scale:

50–60 points	= Excellent player
40–49 points	= Very good player, but there's still room for improvement
30–39 points	= Good player—keep practicing
20–29 points	= Weak player, with *lots* of room for improvement
19 points or less	= Need to return to learning the basics

TEACHER EVALUATION

Now ask your teacher, coach, or trained partner to watch you perform at least three times. The evaluator should record your game responses on the scoresheet below.

Game Scoresheet

Name _____

Place a tally mark by the skill that you observe the student performing within a game situation. Add a slash mark across the tally mark if the student was accurate, also. In the last column, total the scores for all three dates.

For example, say the player serves six times in a game. If four of those serves land in the opponent's court, then the tally marks would look like this: + + + + − −.

Skill	Date	Date	Date	Total ___ of ___
Serve				
Pass				
Set				
Attack				
a. Dink				
b. Off-Speed				
c. Hard-Driven Spike				
Block				
Dig				
Individual Defense				
a. Roll				
b. Sprawl				

Appendix

Individual Program

INDIVIDUAL COURSE IN _____

STUDENT'S NAME _____

GRADE/COURSE SECTION _____

STUDENT ID # _____

SKILLS/CONCEPTS	TECHNIQUE AND PERFORMANCE OBJECTIVES	WT* ×	POINT PROGRESS** 1 2 3 4	=	FINAL SCORE***

Note. From "The Role of Expert Knowledge Structures in an Instructional Design Model for Physical Education" by J.N. Vickers, 1983, *Journal of Teaching in Physical Education,* **2**(3), p. 17. Copyright 1983 by Joan N. Vickers. Adapted by permission.

*WT = Weighting of an objective's degree of difficulty.

**PROGRESS = Ongoing success, which may be expressed in terms of (a) accumulated points (1, 2, 3, 4); (b) grades (D, C, B, A); (c) symbols (merit, bronze, silver, gold); (d) unsatisfactory/satisfactory; and others as desired.

***FINAL SCORE equals WT times PROGRESS.

Suggested Readings

Bertucci, B., & Hippolyte, R. (Eds.) (1984). *Championship volleyball drills* (Vol. I). Champaign, IL: Leisure Press.

Bertucci, B., & Korgut, T. (Eds.) (1985). *Championship volleyball drills* (Vol. II). Champaign, IL: Leisure Press.

Cherebetiu, G. (1969). *Volleyball techniques.* Hollywood, CA: Creative Sports Books.

Coleman, J.E. (1976). *Power volleyball.* North Palm Beach, FL: The Athletic Institute.

Dougherty, N.J. (Ed.) (1983). *Physical education and sport for the secondary school student.* Reston, VA: American Alliance for Health, Physical Education, Recreation and Dance.

Egstrom, G.H., & Schaafsma, F. (1980). *Volleyball* (3rd ed.). Dubuque, IA: Wm. C. Brown.

Ejem, M., Buchtel, J., & Johnson, K.M. (1983). *Contemporary volleyball.* Huntington Beach, CA: Volleyball Plus.

Fraser, S.D. (1988). *Strategies for competitive volleyball.* Champaign, IL: Leisure Press.

Gozansky, S. (1983). *Championship volleyball techniques and drills.* West Nyack, NY: Parker.

International Volleyball Federation coaches manual. (1975). Vanier, ON: Canadian Volleyball Association.

Keller, V. (1977). *Point, game and match.* San Francisco, CA: United States Volleyball Association Publications.

Lucas, J. (1985). *Pass, set, crush volleyball illustrated.* Wenatchee, WA: Euclid Northwest Publications.

Matsudaira, Y. (1977). *Winning volleyball.* Vanier, ON: Canadian Volleyball Association.

Peppler, M.J. (1977). *Inside volleyball for women.* Chicago, IL: Henry Regnery.

Prsala, J. (1971). *Fundamental volleyball contacts.* Vanier, ON: Canadian Volleyball Association.

Sandefur, R. (1970). *Volleyball.* Pacific Palisades, CA: Goodyear.

Scates, A.E. (1984). *Winning volleyball drills.* Boston: Allyn and Bacon.

Scates, A.E. (1976). *Winning volleyball* (2nd ed.). Boston: Allyn and Bacon.

Scates, A.E., & Ward, J. (1975). *Volleyball* (2nd ed.). Boston: Allyn and Bacon.

Selinger, A., & Ackermann-Blount, J. (1986). *Arie Selinger's power volleyball.* New York: St. Martin's Press.

Slaymaker, T., & Brown, V. (1970). *Power volleyball.* Philadelphia: W.B. Saunders.

Smith, R.E. (Ed.) (1987). *United States Volleyball Association official guide.* Colorado Springs, CO: United States Volleyball Association Publications.

Tennent, M. (1977). *Volleyball team play.* Vanier, ON: Canadian Volleyball Association.

Thijpen, J. (1974). *Power volleyball for girls and women* (2nd ed.). Dubque, IA: Wm. C. Brown.

About the Authors

Barbara L. Viera is an associate professor of physical education and the head volleyball coach at the University of Delaware. She has coached and taught volleyball at all levels for over 25 years. Barbara's teams at Delaware have competed successfully at the Division I level, achieving a win/loss record that places her in the top 10 of all-time active Division I winning coaches in the country. Along with her college coaching, Barbara has established and successfully run a junior volleyball program for high school and junior high school players in the state of Delaware.

In addition to teaching and coaching in Delaware, Barbara has written several articles and chapters in books, journals, and newsletters and has made presentations at the regional, national, and international levels. She has taught volleyball in Costa Rica, Guatemala, Panama, Mexico, and Argentina, working with teachers, coaches, national teams, and players of all age levels. Her teams have competed in St. Lucia and Barbados.

Bonnie Jill Ferguson is an assistant professor of physical education and the head coach of the women's softball and tennis teams at the University of Delaware. For over nine years, her responsibilities have included teaching the skills, techniques, and knowledge of volleyball to those studying to be physical education teachers. Bonnie Jill and Barbara have established a competency-based model for teaching volleyball. Through 5 years of competitive playing experience at the collegiate and USVBA levels, Bonnie Jill developed a knowledge and understanding of volleyball, giving her insight into the various aspects of the game from a player's point of view.